INVESTMENT
of a
LIFETIME

A *personal guide*
to investing in your life

K.C. ERICKSON

A BLUE CHIP BOOK
Published by Horizon Investments, L.C.

A BLUE CHIP BOOK
Published by Horizon Investments, L.C.

HORIZON INVESTMENTS, L.C.
P. O. Box 1284
Bountiful, Utah 84011-1284
(801) 294-4430

INVESTMENT OF A LIFETIME

Cover & Book Design
by David Titensor
Printed at Carr Printing Company
Bountiful, Utah

Library of Congress
Cataloging-in-Publication Data

Erickson, K.C.
Investment of a Lifetime: A personal guide to investing in your life/K.C. Erickson

Library of Congress Catalog Card
Number: 96-94869
ISBN:0-9655000-0-4

$\mathcal{A}$CKNOWLEDGEMENTS

Special thanks to all those who have invested their time, effort, and support in making this book possible. To Barry, my investment partner. To Jeff, Inger, Cori, Tory, Scott, Kaysee, Kelli, Kacee, Kristy, and Joshua who are major investments in my life. To my brother, Kent, for his inspiring phone calls. To Dora Flack, my mentor and a master editor. To Betty Van Orden and Eleanor Hoagland for constantly motivating me to complete the manuscript. To Marj Jeppson for her example of dedicated investing. To Jim and Cloy Kent for sharing their talents. To Brian Gubler for his relentless support. To Dave Titensor, Dave Millward and Carr Printing for their creative input and the production of this book. To Horizon: Chad, Jason, Ryan, Craig, and Jeff for their desire to make life better for others.

To My Parents
With gratitude for the
Lifetime Investment
to their family.

TABLE OF CONTENTS

$\mathcal{Y}$OU CAN PUT
MONEY ASIDE AND SAVE IT,
BUT YOU CAN'T PUT *time*
ASIDE FOR FUTURE USE.
YOU EITHER *invest* TIME
OR SPEND IT.

ℐNVESTING ℐN ℒIFE

*W*hether a high-profile CEO, an aspiring professional, or a busy stay-at-home parent, this book is for you, and anyone else who wants to make the most out of life. Wouldn't you like to know how virtually everything you do can add to your wealth of living?

Actually, it is very simple. So simple in fact, that I cannot believe it took me so long to discover this missing piece to one of life's puzzles.

Ever since I was young, I studied people and how money affected their lives. I could not discern the correlation between wealth, success, and happiness and how they affected each other. I knew wealthy people who appeared to have no desire nor ambition to succeed in life. And yet they had the financial means to support most aspirations. Conversely, I studied people who had very little money. Many of them worked hard to succeed financially and to achieve high goals. These same people often appeared to be happy most of the time.

Life's puzzle became more perplexing when I viewed exactly the opposite traits in other people. Why was it that money was a deterrent to some and to others it was a blessing? It did not seem to matter if they were rich or poor. I examined my parents' philosophy concerning money.

My parents were avid savers. They saved during the lean years. And they saved even more when times were good. I watched their savings escalate into a sizable estate. At an early age, I concluded that in order to be successful, you must save.

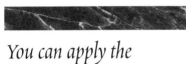

You can apply the investment concept immediately to your personal life.

But my conclusion did not solve the puzzle. Saving money did not always ensure happiness. There still remained a couple of missing pieces.

One missing part was found in the early years of marriage. While trying to save for a house, I soon realized that money does not grow if you merely stash it away and hoard it. You must invest money for financial prosperity. Now there was only one more piece which I had to find to complete the puzzle. I was beginning to understand why saving and investing were vital constituents of financial success. But why were some wealthy people happy and continuously growing while others were miserable and listless?

One afternoon at my desk, while poring over our family's financial statements, the missing piece subtly began to appear. I had learned various ways to "invest" money. What if I "invested" in life in the same manner? Would success result from such action? Would I discover the key to finding happiness, no matter if I were financially wealthy or not?

The idea fascinated me. Immediately, I looked up the word "Invest" in the dictionary. Then I looked up the word "Spend."

Excitement overcame me as though I understood the meanings of those two words for the first time.

Investing my time with intended personal benefits sounded much more enticing than spending, or passing, my time. I decided to begin an investment program in life. I shared my new discovery with a few close friends. My enthusiasm for the concept soared as they experimented with the idea and related personal experiences of how the "investment concept" altered their thinking in a positive way.

Ryan, a young father, shared the following incident:

"My wife called me at work one afternoon. She was in a real dilemma. She had a doctor's appointment and couldn't find anyone to stay with our kids. So she asked me to come home for a couple of hours.

"I looked at my desk covered with work and was really reluctant to ask permission to slip out of the office. But I finally gave in to my wife's pleading and explained to my supervisor that I needed to leave for a few hours.

"As I drove home, I thought about the investment concept. Since I had committed to watch our children, I figured I had two options. I could either invest my time building a relationship with my two little girls or I could merely spend my time tending them while waiting for my wife to return. I decided to test the investment concept.

"What happened? My attitude changed completely. I forgot about my desk covered with papers as I looked forward to my forthcoming investment. I had a great time coloring and playing with my girls, all the time reflecting how I was investing in our relationship. I felt really good as I experienced immediate returns.

"I later realized my investment was far more reaching than I had initially anticipated. My wife really appreciated my help. I actually invested in her at the same time by letting her know that she is more important to me than my work. The investing concept affected all four of us in a beneficial way. I guess you could say, we all reaped dividends."

Similar stories flooded in. Every person who initiated the investment concept experienced immediate returns. And everyone expressed how good they felt inside.

I am convinced that YOU can apply this concept immediately to your own life and begin to reap similar rewards. When you invest, you have a reason to arise each morning with the excitement of greeting new opportunities in life. You sense accomplishment at the end of each day. Your life becomes richer and more meaningful. You begin to dream again.

You might feel as though some of your dreams have faded with the passing of years and the reality of time. Once you initiate the investment concept, you will discover that investing in life paves a way for dreams to resurface and rekindle. You need only to understand how to begin your personal investment program.

Because money is a tangible commodity used nearly every day, you probably already comprehend and utilize several techniques in managing your money and creating new wealth. The amazing fact is that many of the same strategies used in creating financial wealth are similar to those you can use in creating a prosperous personal life.

Adopting an INVESTMENT ATTITUDE is essential. Therefore, you must understand what an INVESTMENT ATTITUDE is and how you can relate it to investing in your life on a daily basis.

The first two chapters of this book detail terms and strategies which are vital for you to know in order to invest in your life. But once you comprehend the simple instructions and the power of this concept, you will be on your way to the most exciting and rewarding investment plan you have ever considered.

May you enjoy the adventure of learning how to invest in your life. There is no limit as to what you can accomplish because you are pursuing:

AN INVESTMENT OF A LIFETIME!

$\mathcal{M}$ANY OF THE SAME STRATEGIES USED IN CREATING FINANCIAL WEALTH ARE SIMILAR TO THOSE YOU CAN USE IN CREATING A PROSPEROUS PERSONAL LIFE.

1

THE *INVESTMENT* *ATTITUDE*

elcome to the world of investing—INVESTING IN LIFE! The most valuable commodities discussed are people and time. In this realm of investing you must realize that money is not the only source of wealth. Many people in this world with very little money are extremely wealthy. On the other hand, there are many people who have amassed great amounts of money and yet their personal lives are miserably impoverished.

The key is learning how to assess your wealth in terms other than money. This requires a change in the thinking process. Visualize the type of life you desire to live and ask yourself, "What does it mean to live a rich life?"

One way to evaluate the above question is to consider your present state. Ask yourself how rich you feel at this very moment. Like most people, you have probably developed a habit of measuring your wealth by the number of digits in your bank account. But remember, your bank account is only a measure of your financial wealth, and this type of wealth is simply a small portion of your life's total net worth.

Consider your wealth in other areas of life. Do you enjoy a rich relationship with your spouse? Are your children more priceless to you than gold? Is your life abundant with good friends? Do you possess a collection of warm memories with parents and siblings? Are your days embellished with the enjoyment of sunsets and the wonders of nature?

The potential of your Personal Wealth is absolutely unlimited. At this point, you should begin to recognize the importance of enhancing and magnifying your definition of wealth. As you begin investing in many different areas of your life, you will become an extremely wealthy person. This is what the concept of developing an INVESTMENT ATTITUDE is all about — learning to invest, rather than spend, your time and effort to create valuable experiences.

By adopting an Investment Attitude, virtually every daily task can add to your wealth of living.

By adopting an INVESTMENT ATTITUDE, virtually every daily task can add to your wealth of living. Each day you will find new ways to invest in your life and make it richer. Do you want to know how this is accomplished? Then prepare yourself for a soul-changing quest toward developing an INVESTMENT ATTITUDE and becoming a true investor in life.

By understanding the meaning of three words and utilizing the concepts encompassing each one, you will be on your way to developing an INVESTMENT ATTITUDE. The words you must comprehend are *invest*, *spend*, and *save*. Although you may typically use these terms when creating a financial budget or portfolio, they can also be applied to your personal life investment plan.

Consider the word INVEST. "Financial investing" is putting money to a use expected to yield a profit. Investing in your life is putting time to a use expected to yield a benefit or an improvement in your life.

In contrast, when you SPEND financial resources, you pay out money and exhaust your capital. Likewise, when you spend life's vital resource, you merely pass time and deplete it.

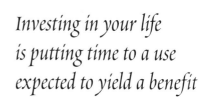

Investing is building and creating wealth, not exhausting it by spending. An INVESTMENT ATTITUDE shifts your thought processes into building and creating which directs you away from spending.

Investing in your life is putting time to a use expected to yield a benefit or an improvement in your life.

For this reason, many financial advisors council you to adopt an investing mentality.

Another word which relates well to investing is SAVE. When you save money, you put it aside for the future instead of spending it immediately.

As stated previously, this book is not about investing money. INVESTMENT OF A LIFETIME deals with investing in your life. Review the meaning of the following three words and consider how they can relate to your present state of living.

INVEST: TO PUT MONEY, OR TIME, TO A USE
      EXPECTED TO YIELD A PROFIT.

SPEND: TO PAY OUT MONEY, TO PASS TIME.

SAVE: TO PUT MONEY ASIDE FOR FUTURE
USE RATHER THAN USING IT FOR
IMMEDIATE SPENDING.

Isn't it interesting that you can put money aside and save it, but you cannot put TIME aside for future use? You either INVEST time or SPEND it. This is why developing an INVESTMENT ATTITUDE is so crucial in life.

The investing world is an exciting sphere because the word "invest" denotes positive thought in action. An INVESTMENT ATTITUDE is synonymous with a positive attitude. Why? Much like a positive attitude, the benefits of an INVESTMENT ATTITUDE are realized only to the extent it is developed and maintained. For this reason, it is important to establish a long-term perspective which often requires sacrificing immediate desires. By focusing on long-term benefits and rewards, an INVESTMENT ATTITUDE is much easier to maintain.

Maintaining and sustaining an INVESTMENT ATTITUDE is the key to a successful financial investment plan. Similarly, it is the key to a successful LIFE investment plan. An INVESTMENT ATTITUDE is the golden thread running through both concepts which enables you to invest in your life the same way you invest in the financial markets.

Investing in the financial markets can be quite an experience. If you have ever been on Wall Street, or even read the famous "Journal" bearing its name, you have probably noticed that financial investors have a language all their own. Although this language can be somewhat confusing at times, there are only a few terms you must know when creating your personal life investment plan.

One of the objectives of this book is to define some very basic words and concepts frequently used in the financial world and to show how they relate to investing in your life. Once you understand these necessary terms and ideas, you will be taught a few simple strategies used by successful financial planners. These strategies will also relate to investing in your life.

Armed with this information, you will discover easy ways to make your life richer and more rewarding as you create your PERSONAL LIFE PORTFOLIO (PLP).

You can put money aside and save it, but you cannot put TIME aside for future use. You either INVEST time or SPEND it.

You do not have to be a financial wizard to invest in your life. Believe it or not, once you have read the following chapter, you will be prepared to create your PERSONAL LIFE PORTFOLIO and begin your personal life investment program. Once your investment program commences, you will recognize that many of your investments generate immediate returns. Typically, that is a great deal more than the financial world can promise you!

The majority of investments discussed deal with investing in people. When your life is rich with those you love and you experience positive moments with them, you usually sense an abundance of zest and enthusiasm. The more you invest in such areas, your life experiences become richer and you feel better within.

The stunning characteristic of this concept is that by investing time and effort in those you love (and want to love), your investments yield noticeable dividends and you acquire significant returns of love.

Most financially wealthy people devote much time and thought to creating and building their monetary investments. As previously stated, the strategies for investing in your life are simple and basic. But you must be willing to invest your time and effort in establishing your personal investment program. If you accept the challenge, your life will change dramatically.

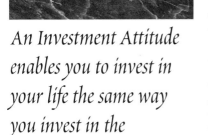

An Investment Attitude enables you to invest in your life the same way you invest in the financial markets.

No longer will menial tasks drive you crazy and cause stress. With stress being blamed as one of the leading causes of disease and death in our country, it is probably one element you wish to eliminate.

Rather than "spending" time and allowing stress to overtake you, why not learn how to "invest" your time and effort toward creating a richer and more rewarding life?

The following chapter will help you begin a personal investment plan. You will learn how to make investments in your PERSONAL LIFE PORTFOLIO. By investing a little time and effort in learning the simple techniques presented, you will realize generous returns associated with investing in life. After you complete Chapter 2 and know how to set up your life investment plan, you will soar through the following pages of exciting ideas.

The succeeding chapters will provide suggestions and guidelines for investing in areas which will interest you. You will realize the importance of investing in your physical well-being and development, as well as in your mental and spiritual wellness. This investment is your Personal Growth.

You will awake to the need of investing heavily in your Spouse and be reminded of the generous returns available. Your sensitivity to the intrinsic value of your Children will magnify as you decide how to invest time with them.

Your Profession or Career will denote a deeper significance as you contemplate its role in life. You will be sharply cognizant of Friends who have influenced you and made your life rich and purposeful. They will become a part of your investment plan.

You do not have to be a financial wizard to invest in your life.

By the time you finish reading this book, you will recognize the overwhelming potential of a life geared toward investing as opposed to a life squandered in spending. The concept will relate to nearly everything you do. Your existence will take on new meaning and purpose as your INVESTMENT ATTITUDE leads you into a redesigned passage of personal progress.

Let's begin your life-changing journey by discussing the necessary basic terms and concepts that must be understood.

First, what is a portfolio and how do you create your PERSONAL LIFE PORTFOLIO, or your PLP?

$\mathcal{M}$AINTAINING
AND SUSTAINING AN
INVESTMENT ATTITUDE IS
THE KEY TO A SUCCESSFUL
FINANCIAL INVESTMENT
PLAN. SIMILARLY, IT IS THE
KEY TO A SUCCESSFUL LIFE
INVESTMENT PLAN.

2
CREATING *Y*OUR
*P*ERSONAL *L*IFE *P*ORTFOLIO (*PLP*)

financial portfolio is a collection of investments from which you expect a profit or income.

Your PERSONAL LIFE PORTFOLIO (PLP) lists all the valuable personal investments which you expect to benefit your life.

By listing all your investments in a financial portfolio, you can easily be reminded of your monetary investments and also have a record of their activities. The reason for creating a PERSONAL LIFE PORTFOLIO is to have a record of the areas which are valuable and meaningful in your life. This record helps provide direction in making wise use of each day by allowing you to know which areas require your attention and time.

First, let's discuss how to create a financial portfolio which has the possibility of yielding an income. This will help you understand the relationship between a financial portfolio and your PERSONAL LIFE PORTFOLIO. The purpose of creating a portfolio is to diversify assets so everything is not invested in one area.

To diversify your monetary investments means to invest in many different areas that have varying degrees of risk. For example, if all your money is invested in one area such as stocks, and the stock market plunged, your portfolio would suffer a huge loss. In fact, if you had all of your money invested in a single stock, your portfolio could fold completely if that particular company failed. In contrast, if you invested in a number of different stocks, bonds, treasury bills, and other securities, the chances of your portfolio dissolving would be reduced dramatically. Remember the old adage of not putting all your eggs in one basket?

Diversify means "to invest in many different areas which have varying degrees of risk."

The same holds true when creating your PERSONAL LIFE PORTFOLIO. If all your time and energy are invested in a single area, such as your career, you are exposed to a tremendous amount of risk. Because you have neglected other areas, you are left with an unbalanced life and nothing to support you, should your career take a turn for the worst. Consider the status of your PERSONAL LIFE PORTFOLIO should your company suddenly downsize and you were to lose your job. With your career being the only area of investment, your portfolio could completely collapse.

Throughout its history, the stock market has had its ups and downs. The analogy can be drawn between the market and life. You have probably already experienced life's roller coaster ride. Keep this analogy in mind when creating your PERSONAL LIFE PORTFOLIO. Your investments will inevitably take turns in escalating and plunging. However, by diversifying investments, your PERSONAL LIFE PORTFOLIO will remain solid and far less susceptible to the risk of depletion.

Consider again the career investment as an example, but now imagine it being just one of many investments in your portfolio. If your career were to take a dive, the dividends and returns earned in other areas of life will help balance your portfolio and keep it solvent.

To further illustrate this point, may I share a rather somber story about Sara, a young woman whose personal portfolio would have likely dissolved had she not invested in several different areas of her life.

Even at an early age, Sara made a conscious effort to keep her life balanced. She invested wisely in her education and graduated early from college. She was considered by many of her peers to have everything in the world going for her. While attending the university, she met "Mr. Right." They had a story-book romance and wedding. Life could not have been more perfect. However, Sara's seemingly flawless world soon turned upside down.

A year and a half into their marriage, "Mr. Right" decided he had made a wrong decision. He rationalized that he needed more space—alone. Although Sara continued to invest all she could into saving their marriage, her husband was unwilling to make the same investment. After three months of struggling with the idea, she finally submitted to signing papers for a divorce. Heartbroken, Sara moved back to her parents' home. Fortunately, she had invested heavily in her Personal Growth and during this trying time, she relied upon her physical and mental health to keep her going.

Then, right when Sara seemed to be recovering from the loss of her marriage, more tragedy struck. Sara's mother was killed in a car accident. Her life nearly shattered. She and her mother had shared a warm and close relationship. Now, two of the people whom she had held the dearest to her were gone. Sara's entire personal portfolio seemed to be taking a fatal nose dive. However, at this time when life seemed darkest, the other investments in her portfolio began yielding dividends.

Sara had always made it a point to invest her time and effort in many different areas of her life. Dividends from good health were not the only returns her PERSONAL LIFE PORTFOLIO offered. Because of her devotion to her family members, they rallied together, providing comfort and strength to each other. Neighbors and relatives whom Sara had helped in their times of need now rendered support and encouragement. Sara had invested faithfully in her religion, and her religious leaders added assistance by helping restore Sara's hope. They counseled her to pray and she discovered spiritual strength on her knees. Friends with whom Sara had shared many of her life's dreams and aspirations gathered around her and reassured her that she was not alone. Those in whom she had invested diligently provided invaluable returns.

Because Sara had diversified her life's portfolio, she survived her challenging ordeal. In fact, Sara is still consistently investing in her PLP. Once again, she is poised for future growth and prosperity.

PERSONAL LIFE PORTFOLIO

INVESTMENT GOAL

INVESTMENT FORECAST

Month:

Week of:		Sunday	Monday	Tuesday	Wednesday	Thursday	Friday	Saturday	Rating
Investment	Goals								

(Fig. 1)

Now that you understand the importance of investing in several areas, it is time to create your PERSONAL LIFE PORTFOLIO.

On the previous page (Fig. 1) is a facsimile of the tear out sheet located at the back of this book. Gently remove the tear out sheet and use it to follow along as you are presented the seven easy steps to creating your PERSONAL LIFE PORTFOLIO. You may want to make a photo copy of the tear out sheet before marking it up and keep it as your master copy for future use.

As the following instructions are given, fill in the corresponding areas on the sheet. By the time you finish this chapter, you will have created a life investment plan that will be invaluable to you. Let's begin with Step 1.

STEP ONE
CREATE YOUR GOAL

The first step in creating your PERSONAL LIFE PORTFOLIO is to determine your GOAL or your investment objective. This is similar to creating a personal mission statement.

Nearly every business creates a mission statement which designates its specific purpose and aim. Many businesses publish that statement in the front of their annual reports distributed to shareholders. They also display it in other ways in order to acquaint clients, as well as employees, with the company's intentions.

In fact, when I recently made a visit to an ailing friend, I noticed the hospital's Mission Statement posted inside the elevator. By keeping the mission statement in a visible place, it becomes a constant reminder of the hospital's desired goals.

Formulating goals is not always easy. Sometimes it helps to view what others have written. To help you get started, an example is provided below. (See Fig. 2) Take ample time to establish your goal and to decide what you want to achieve by investing in your life.

"I will invest my time wisely in the areas
of life which are most important to me.
Every week I will evaluate my results and realize
the areas in which I must invest more time. I will be
enthusiastic with each investment whether it reaps
a dividend or suffers a downturn. I will maintain
an 'Investment Attitude' in my daily living."

(Fig. 2)

Once you have established your GOAL, write it down in the space provided on your PLP Worksheet under INVEST-MENT GOAL.

You will find that parts of your goal may change from time to time. That is all right. The important thing is that you periodically review your investment objective and evaluate whether you are investing your time rather than spending it.

Now that you have established your goal, you will want to predict the many returns and benefits which will be added to your life as you implement your intentions.

STEP TWO

WRITE YOUR FORECAST

The second step in creating a successful life investment plan is to develop your FORECAST. Forecasting is simply predicting the outcome of your investing efforts. To do this, you must envision in your mind the eventual payoffs associated with investing in life. By forecasting what you hope to gain, your INVESTMENT ATTITUDE will heighten. It is almost like dangling the carrot in front of the horse. When you become discouraged, or when one of your investments takes a sudden downturn, simply study your goal and forecast, and motivation for continued investing will return.

Again, if you are having difficulty on this assignment, following is an example that may help you get started. (See Fig. 3) Allow sufficient time to map out in your mind what you anticipate to gain. Once you feel comfortable with the forecast, write it down in the space provided on your PLP Worksheet under INVESTMENT FORECAST.

INVESTMENT FORECAST

"The investments I make today will yield valuable dividends in years to come because I have selected quality 'Blue Chip' investments with unlimited potential. My life will be rich and abundant because it will be focused on people rather than on things."

(Fig. 3)

By having your Investment Goal and Forecast constantly visible at the top of your PLP Worksheet, they will serve as persistent reminders to help you keep investing.

Maintaining an INVESTMENT ATTITUDE is one of the biggest challenges in sustaining a successful PERSONAL LIFE PORTFOLIO. Remember from Chapter 1, an INVESTMENT ATTITUDE is the

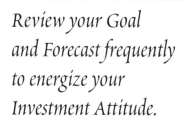

Review your Goal and Forecast frequently to energize your Investment Attitude.

"Golden Thread" of success. Therefore, review your goal and forecast frequently to energize your INVESTMENT ATTITUDE and to remind yourself of intended achievements and future returns.

STEP THREE
RECORD THE DATE

After writing your goal and forecast, it is important to record the date on your PLP Worksheet. In the space provided next to "Week of," directly above the Goals column, write in the current date. Then fill in the appropriate dates in the spaces provided directly under each corresponding day.

The recorded dates on your PLP Worksheet will help you keep a detailed log of your investing activities. Past PLP Worksheets can be periodically referred to for evaluation purposes in which you can compare past and present investing performance. The dates also serve as reminders of special days or events that occur during a particular week.

Notice this sheet is for a week's investments. This is not a day-planner. Remember you are investing, not simply marking things off a "to-do" list. The habit of making lists often leads you into a "spending" mode of thinking. You "spend" time at the grocery store buying food. You come home and scratch off one more task you have completed for the day.

With an INVESTMENT ATTITUDE, you also must purchase groceries at the store. But when you consider your trip to the store as a way to invest in your personal health, as well as the health of your spouse and children, your grocery shopping takes on an entirely new meaning. Suddenly, you want to "invest" quality time shopping for healthy food because you value your health and the health of others who will be affected. With an INVESTMENT ATTITUDE, grocery shopping evolves into an important investment rather than a duty or chore.

STEP FOUR
LIST PREFERRED INVESTMENTS

The fourth step in creating your PERSONAL LIFE PORTFOLIO is to select your PREFERRED INVESTMENTS. Most financial planners suggest allowing ample time to weigh each possibility when constructing a financial portfolio. They also suggest studying each option and reading a prospectus before purchasing. If you plan to put your hard-earned money into a stock or an investment, you should know what you are buying.

The same advice pertains to setting up your PERSONAL LIFE PORTFOLIO as well. Rather than studying a prospectus, however, you must consider the areas of your life which are most important. Ask yourself questions such as, "What means the most to me?" "Who means the most to me?" "What makes me happy?" "What do I enjoy most in life?"

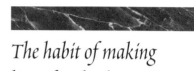

The habit of making lists often leads you into a "spending" mode of thinking.

When determining your investment areas, take your time. Your personal life investments become much more valuable than your financial investments.

In the stock market, if one stock turns out to be a real loser, you might decide to dump it, take a loss and search for another investment.

Your PERSONAL LIFE PORTFOLIO is not quite that easy to manipulate. Again, consider the example of investing in marriage. Recall the pain and heartache Sara experienced when her husband decided to stop investing in their relationship. If he had been willing to invest, their marriage would have likely survived. If your spouse takes a real downturn, hopefully you will not give up and abandon your investment like Sara's husband did. Instead, you must consider your spouse to be one of your Blue Chip investments.

In the stock market, blue chips are stocks of the largest, most consistently profitable corporations. They are highly valued in the market.

In your PERSONAL LIFE PORTFOLIO, it is wise to include stable Blue Chip investments, such as your spouse. These investments not only add stability, but are also characterized by their potential for unlimited growth. Nevertheless, you must remember that in the stock market, even Blue Chips have their downturns. With this understanding you are well advised to maintain a long-term perspective of consistent investing. In other words, keep cultivating your INVESTMENT ATTITUDE.

Your personal life investments become much more valuable than your financial investments.

Always keep in mind that your portfolio must be diversified. To begin diversifying, take time to list the areas in your life which have the highest value. List as many as you can.

Here is an example of five investments you may want to consider: (Each of these investments will be explored in later chapters.)

VALUABLE INVESTMENTS
- ⚖ Personal Growth
- ⚖ Spouse
- ⚖ Children
- ⚖ Profession
- ⚖ Friends

It is not necessary to determine which of your investments is most valuable. Your investments are not competing with each other. In your PERSONAL LIFE PORTFOLIO you will discover that each investment is priceless in and of itself. In fact, you may realize there are many synergies between investments in your PLP. (By now you should be well acquainted with your

PERSONAL LIFE PORTFOLIO. Henceforth, it will be referred to as your PLP.)

Now refer again to your tear out sheet.

Go to the column under INVESTMENTS. Here you will list your valued investments. One suggestion is to place your Personal Growth investment in the top square to remind you of its

"Blue Chip" investments are valued for their stability and their potential for unlimited growth.

significance to your entire portfolio. The importance of this particular investment will be addressed in Chapter Three.

STEP FIVE
WRITE INDIVIDUAL INVESTMENT GOALS

Once you have listed your investments, you must establish a GOAL for each one. At the right of each investment, write down your goal for that area.

Setting goals for each investment area is exciting. You force yourself to project toward the future. Your vision broadens as you contemplate each investment's unlimited potential.

For example, when considering the investment in your children, you visualize five, ten, fifteen years down the line and you begin to recognize possibilities of vast growth and accomplishment. Your enthusiasm soars as you anticipate future returns. Although you realize there will be obstacles along the way, your goals encourage you to keep a long-term

By actually writing down your goals, you are reaffirming intentions to create a richer and more rewarding life.

perspective of consistent investing. Your goals keep your investing strategies on track and fire up your INVESTMENT ATTITUDE.

Remember, your PLP is yours, so write goals as they pertain to personal needs and ambitions. By actually writing down your goals, you are reaffirming intentions to create a richer and more rewarding life. Written goals are a necessary part of creating your PLP.

STEP SIX
RECORD INVESTING ACTIVITIES

The next step is to record your INVESTING ACTIVITIES. Beginning with the first day, Sunday, initiate your investment program. Determine your responsibilities or appointments for that day. If they fall into any of your investment areas, write them down. Now list all your appointments and obligations for the rest of the week in the appropriate areas. As days begin to fill with obligations, appointments and activities, you will readily see which investment areas tend to require the most time and effort.

You will also recognize which investment areas have few, if any, investments projected for the coming week. Consider ways to invest in those areas. Even with only one investment a week, by year's end you would accumulate 52 deposits in your priceless investment. The concept of consistent investing is a key to creating and building your PLP.

Initiating plans for consistent investing in the most important areas of life will increase and sustain your INVESTMENT ATTITUDE. That golden thread will weave itself throughout your weekly activities, demonstrating the inestimable value of investing time and effort wisely.

Undoubtedly, some appointments will not seem to fit in any of your investment areas. These appointments can be recorded at the bottom of the page under the appropriate day. However, you will eventually realize that nearly everything you do during the day and week can be utilized as a way to create and build your PLP— if you maintain an INVESTMENT ATTITUDE.

Many ordinary activities are quickly transformed into golden opportunities of investing when an investing mentality is adopted.

As an example, consider a husband who invests in his wife by doing the dishes after each meal—a seemingly mundane chore. However, the completed task is not as important as the message it sends to his wife— that he values her time as much as his own. He senses an instant reward in knowing that he has invested in someone he loves. Additionally, his appreciative wife may feel inclined to return additional dividends by doing something nice for him. The rewards can truly be compounding.

Note that an INVESTMENT ATTITUDE develops over a period of time. If sustained and nurtured, it will eventually become a way of life which is rich with dividends.

By now you are beginning to catch a glimpse of the unlimited possibilities for your PLP. Each day takes on new meaning as you decide where you will invest your time.

STEP SEVEN
TRACK YOUR INVESTMENTS

Another necessary strategy in wise investing is tracking your investments. TRACKING is simply keeping an up-to-date record of investing activities.

By keeping a record of your investments, you will be able to recognize the areas which are doing well and those which are in need of heavier deposits.

At the end of the week, hopefully you will have made many contributions to your PLP. Evaluate the status of each investment area and assess the quality of contributions to each one.

Your PLP is one of the easiest and surest ways of evaluating progress in life.

You are the only one who can provide this evaluation because only you know how each investment is progressing and what contributes to its growth. Be honest.

This is merely an evaluation. You are competing with no one. Your main desire is to learn how to invest wisely in your PLP so each valuable investment has the opportunity for growth. You will discover that your PLP is one of the easiest and surest ways of evaluating progress in life.

For those who would like to take the evaluation process one step further, assess the time and effort invested in each area by using the following rating system:

RATING	PERFORMANCE
6	Highest Effort
5	Excellent Effort
4	Good Effort
3	Medium Effort
2	Some Effort
1	Little Effort
0	No Effort

Under the column RATING, write the number which indicates the quality level of investing efforts during the week. Again, remember you are competing with no one. This is solely for your personal information.

Some weeks you will record several 6's because of high investing. Other weeks may show several areas of 3's and 2's because more attention was required by other investments.

Totaling up the weekly rating of each investment area every three months provides a quarterly report which can be used to evaluate your PLP and the status of each valuable investment. You will then know where most of your time and effort has been invested. This will help you determine if there are highly valued areas where you are not yet investing enough time and concern.

You may consider compiling your quarterly reports into a yearly statement. In so doing, you would have on record a complete year stating your investment activities. What an incredible way to track your life!

Now take a few moments and review the primary steps in creating your PLP.

STEP 1 - Create your PLP GOAL

STEP 2 - Write your FORECAST

STEP 3 - Record Month and Week

STEP 4 - List PREFERRED INVESTMENTS

STEP 5 - Write Investment Area GOALS

STEP 6 - Record your INVESTING ACTIVITIES

STEP 7 - TRACK your investments

Refer to Appendix for examples of completed PLP Worksheets

As promised, you are now prepared to create your PLP. You have the knowledge and the skills. As you begin to formulate investment areas and goals, consider the following chapters. Here you will be introduced to a variety of worthwhile investments. Many ideas will be presented on *how* to invest in each one, *why* the investment is valuable and *where* the projected returns can lead.

One of the most valued areas of investment is
PERSONAL GROWTH.

*I*NVESTING IN
PERSONAL GROWTH IS
SIMILAR TO INVESTING IN
A HIGH-YIELD, LONG-TERM
TREASURY BOND. IT IS
A SOLID, RISK FREE
INVESTMENT.

3

PERSONAL GROWTH INVESTMENT

O f all the investments in your PLP, none are more important than Personal Growth. Investment in this area can be considered the risk-free portion of your portfolio. In many ways, investing in Personal Growth is similar to investing in a high-yield, long-term Treasury Bond.

The returns on a U.S. Treasury Bond are guaranteed by the U.S. Government and the investment is virtually risk free. You might not comprehend at first how your Personal Growth compares to a risk-free investment. But as you read this chapter, you will be astonished at the similarities, one of them being stability.

Personal Growth is a solid and vital investment. No matter how valid and rewarding other investments might be, if you lose health and life, your PLP dissolves. On the other hand, remember this is only one part of your overall investment plan. Use wisdom in the type of investment made in this area.

Some people mistakenly believe that if you invest in yourself, you INDULGE in yourself. Indulging and investing are two very different venues. When you indulge, you allow yourself gratification and slide easily into narcissism. (Recall that

Narcissus was a young Greek god who was extremely handsome and he was very proud of his own beauty. He fell in love with his own reflection in a pool of clear water. He was so much in love with himself that he could not leave the pool. At last he died and was changed into the flower we now call the narcissus.)

Investing in yourself provides opportunity for growth and stability. As you invest quality time and effort in this portion of your portfolio, you will be required to accept and appreciate your own needs and ambitions.

Investing in yourself provides opportunity for growth and stability.

Needs do not always coincide with desires. As a part of Personal Growth, consider investing in a good physical fitness routine, even if you do not enjoy physical activity.

Countless reports advocate taking time for exercise. Experts have proven that an active person is healthier and usually possesses more vitality. Those two returns alone should warrant investment in this area. With enhanced energy and stamina, your entire PLP will benefit.

For those who enjoy physical activity, guilt of taking time from pressing matters can play a major role in neglecting your body's needs. Guilt alone can prevent you from taking a stimulating walk or engaging in an exercise program because there are so many other tasks waiting to be accomplished. But this important facet of life must not be neglected.

The following excerpt illustrates the importance of this investment:

"AS MANY AS 12% OF ALL DEATHS—250,000 PER YEAR—
IN THE U.S. MAY BE ATTRIBUTED INDIRECTLY TO LACK OF
REGULAR PHYSICAL ACTIVITY. ALL IT TAKES IS MODERATE
ACTIVITY, SUCH AS BRISK WALKING, FOR 30 MINUTES FIVE
TIMES A WEEK, OR STRENUOUS EXERCISE FOR 20 MINUTES
THREE TIMES A WEEK."

UNIVERSITY OF CALIFORNIA AT BERKELEY,

WELLNESS LETTER, VOL. 11 JUNE, 1995

Studies have shown that physical activity helps control weight, lower blood pressure, and reduce stress. Incorporating exercise into a Personal Growth investment affects both physical and mental abilities.

With abundant energy to accomplish more tasks and an acute mentality to maintain a positive attitude, your entire PLP will benefit.

Once convinced of the need for physical activity, create your own exercise program. Acknowledge personal likes and dislikes. You might enjoy walking or jogging. Or perhaps you are a swimmer and enjoy early morning workouts at the pool. Maybe working out with others in a gym would be preferred. Or you may be more comfortable in your own home following an aerobics program on TV or using one of the many exercise machines now available on the market.

The choice is yours. Make it enjoyable. Remember, you are not creating an exercise program to impress friends or neighbors. You are investing in a part of your Personal Growth with aspirations of acquiring generous returns in good health.

As you exercise, keep in mind your investment objective. With an INVESTMENT ATTITUDE, you will no longer feel guilty taking time out of a busy schedule to exercise. Instead of "spending" time just working up a sweat, you are now "investing" time in Personal Growth.

However, exercise is only a portion of this investment. Many doctors suggest that health is more than absence of physical disease. Health involves body, mind and spirit.

Many doctors suggest that health is more than absence of physical disease. Health involves body, mind and spirit.

Many years ago, a book hit the market entitled, *The Power of Positive Thinking.* It became increasingly popular, selling over fifteen million copies. What caused the book's phenomenal success?

The book was written by Norman Vincent Peale who was a well-known lecturer and writer of inspirational material. But it was not entirely Peale's style of writing which sold the millions of copies. It was his message.

His chapter titles captured people's interest.

"BELIEVE IN YOURSELF"
"A PEACEFUL MIND GENERATES POWER"
"HOW TO HAVE CONSTANT ENERGY"
"HOW TO GET PEOPLE TO LIKE YOU"

Those are just a few of his subjects. In his many books he related story after story of how people's health was renewed when inner peace was discovered. He shared true stories of spiritual victory even when the physical body failed.

In a world of intense competition and high-tech skills, an optimistic and positive attitude is necessary just to keep going each day. As you invest in your physical adeptness, invest in mind and spirit as well.

You might want to set a goal of reading books or articles which remind you of the importance of thinking positive thoughts. Or if that does not appeal to you, select books which stimulate deep thought and provide reason to ponder. Benefit yourself by reading materials of interest which furnish an ongoing education for your mind.

For example, if you desire to become an entrepreneur with the aspirations of someday starting your own business, read about successful people who have accomplished that dream. Many high-profile entrepreneurs have written books or autobiographies that provide insight and suggestions depicting ways of following their paths of success. Take time to read what they have to say.

Here again, you might experience guilt taking time out of a frenzied schedule to read. Push those feelings aside and remember that you are investing in your PLP. Reading is to your mind what exercise is to your physical body.

As you read books by authors who have successfully achieved their dreams, these people can often serve as mentors by revealing their secrets of success. One such example is Anthony Robbins. He has written numerous books which tell how he achieved prosperity, and he does not hesitate to share his secrets of attainment. His books stimulate the mind. When you can learn from those who have become what you aspire to be, why not take advantage of the opportunity?

Stephen R. Covey, the author of *The Seven Habits of Highly Effective People,* is another example of one who has discovered some of the secrets of success. The title of his book conveys what a stimulating investment it can be. If you desire to become a so-called "highly effective person," invest ample time in reading and learning from Covey's experiences and teachings.

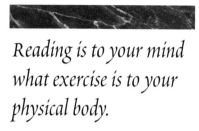

Reading is to your mind what exercise is to your physical body.

If your interests lie in art or music, read about those who have achieved greatness in these areas. In addition, consider investing some of your time brushing shoulders with those who share your interests. You will be surprised how rejuvenated you feel just by being in their presence.

Perhaps you have an innate desire to paint. Read about, or better yet, make an effort to meet someone who can become your mentor. Study the daily schedule, the habits, and the goals your mentor has developed over the years. There are many great artists who possess an intrinsic desire to pass on what they have learned to those who are interested in their work.

One such artist is Cloy Kent, a well-known portrait painter who has been commissioned to paint portraits of numerous prominent and famous people throughout the world. Over the course of her life, she has become an inspiration to many. She is respected for her talent and known for her enthusiasm and positive attitude toward life. Even in the worst of times, Cloy somehow maintains a cheerful outlook on life.

She once shared her secret of cultivating and preserving her positive attitude. When asked if she ever encountered a down day, she smiled and said, "Of course I have my bad days. In fact, I sometimes even give in to feeling sorry for myself. When I recognize myself in one of these negative states, I look at the clock and allow fifteen minutes for a 'pity-party.' I can pout, complain and even cry if I want. But at the end of fifteen minutes, I tell myself it's all over and I must get on with my work."

Cloy Kent is a vibrant individual who has invested heavily in her love of art. But she has also invested wisely in several other areas which provide her a wealth of stimulation for an active life. She recently celebrated her Golden Wedding anniversary with her sweetheart. Six children continue to provide many rich returns. Her list of friends is long. Many people have asked her if she has considered writing a personal biography. If she ever does, it would be well worth the time to read.

Meeting, or even reading about people like this can influence your life dramatically. In fact, reading biographies can be one of the best sharpening tools available in keeping an alert and bright mind. Many people have overcome great obstacles to achieve their dreams. Reading about their personal lives can provide inspiration and valuable insight to many of life's challenges.

Once you have determined to keep your mind alert and your body active, consider your spiritual growth. Spiritual means, "of, or relating to the soul or spirit . . . relating to religious or sacred matters."

The older you grow, the more you sense the need of understanding and nourishing spiritual well-being. You may be faced with extremely difficult trials someday, with a burden heavier than you ever anticipated. At those times, you will be grateful for having invested in spiritual growth because you will call upon strength which will have to come from within.

Your spiritual power and strength assures freedom from failure. Even though you may be stripped of all belongings, with steadfast spiritual fortitude, you will endure and conquer.

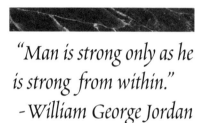

"Man is strong only as he is strong from within."
-William George Jordan

How do you invest in your spiritual growth? Here again, you can read and study experiences about people who have illustrated great spiritual strength. Attend religious services. Read holy or sacred books. Do not be afraid to acknowledge the sensitive feelings within. Recognize the moments when you feel "in-tune" with a Greater Power.

Reach out and extend love to all. Do not hesitate to love the weak, the old, or the little children. By loving others and extending kindness to them, your spiritual strength will increase.

How do you love? Be kind. Be thoughtful. Be generous. Be forgiving. Be courteous.

This type of love is on a much higher level than what our society deems love to be today. Many people identify love as being merely affection and sexual desire. The higher degree of love, however, equates with God's regard for his creations.

You will come to understand that you must love yourself in order to love others. By loving yourself, you will be able to forgive personal shortcomings and failures and have the ability to forgive those around you.

You will become less competitive and more compassionate. You will develop selflessness. You will want to serve more than to be served. You will recognize the intrinsic value of every soul. How you treat other people is often an indication of the relationship you have with yourself. Therefore, invest time in learning how to appreciate who and what you are.

Another dividend of learning to love yourself and mankind will be your ability to appreciate others and their unique roles in life. You will assume responsibility for your own actions and resolve to blame no one else for your present circumstances. This step alone will lift many heavy burdens, leaving your soul free to grow.

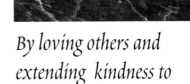

By loving others and extending kindness to them, your spiritual strength will increase.

Investments in spirituality align you with God. You will experience a marvelous return of His gift of creativity as your heart and mind soar to higher plateaus.

When a mind is free to soar, innate creativity flourishes. The more you create, the closer you feel to God. The closer you feel to God, the more you appreciate His goodness and mercy and His creations.

Take time to be alone and experience sublime moments in communicating with God. Some people enjoy meditating. Others build spiritual fortitude by attending religious services. Even solitary walks in nature provide moments to experience a closeness with the Divine.

Since this is your investment, you will discover your own strategy for investing. As you invest wisely in this area, you will be better prepared to manage the volatile swings of other investments in your PLP.

How you treat other people is often an indication of the relationship you have with yourself.

By now, you should realize the importance of investing in Personal Growth. Perhaps you also realize that you often neglect this important aspect of your life's portfolio. However, with an INVESTMENT ATTITUDE, this will change.

Rather than experiencing feelings of selfishness and guilt when doing something good for yourself, you will now prioritize many of these things as important investments in your life. Hopefully, you will consider investments in your Personal Growth to be among the most important activities for each week.

Remember, without a healthy mind, body, and spirit, your PLP will deplete and eventually cease to exist. Therefore, because this investment is so important to your entire portfolio, as you list your investments on your weekly PLP worksheet, you should consider placing Personal Growth at the top of the list.

Consider many years from now. Not only will you be grateful for substantial investments in Personal Growth, your heirs will also be very appreciative. You do not want to burden your children with the task of caring for an invalid parent. Let them bask in the joys of an aging parent who can continue to invest in life.

By consistently investing in Personal Growth, you virtually guarantee rich returns not only for yourself, but for those whom you love. In this respect, the Personal Growth investment can truly be compared to a U. S. Treasury Bond, for they are both considered risk-free investments, yielding guaranteed returns.

Now it is time to consider another investment. . . a true Blue Chip Stock!

Your spouse must be considered your blue chip stock!

4
SPOUSE INVESTMENT

Anyone who is married knows that an argument with your husband or wife in the morning can ruin an entire day. The degree to how greatly the argument affects you lies in direct proportion to how intimate and close the relationship. The more you care about someone, the more you can be hurt by a careless word or action.

The opposite is also true. The stronger the affection and love for one another, the greater joy you will receive from your marriage.

When investing in this portion of your PLP, be generous. This investment directly affects your Personal Growth. If you decide to add children to your portfolio, this investment becomes invaluable. Therefore, your spouse must be considered your Blue Chip Stock!

Do you recall reading about Blue Chip Stocks at the first of the book? You might find it interesting to note that in the early history of the stock market, the term "Blue Chip" was introduced to mean the stocks of the largest, most consistently profitable corporations. The term comes from the blue chips used in poker which are the most valuable chips.

Financial investors realize the merit of such stocks and invest in them for their security and stability as well as their potential for growth and dividends.

Caution! Investing in the stock market is not for the faint-hearted. There are a lot of ups and downs. But if you want the best return, the stock market has historically been the way to go. That is, if you think *long-term*.

You should not invest in the stock market thinking you will jump out if the market falls. History has proven that a correction in the market is always lurking around the corner. Those who profit most in the stock market are those determined souls who can ride the ups and downs and patiently wait out the inevitable corrections or downturns.

Jumping in and out, trying to find the BEST TIMES to invest does not work in either the stock market or in a marriage.

The investors who usually come out with less profits in the market are the "market-timers." They try to time the market as to the best time to jump in or out. Up until now, no one has mastered or discovered the means of consistently and profitably accomplishing this. Bear this in mind as you reflect upon your marriage.

There are inevitable downturns in a marriage which might cause the faint-hearted person to pull out or escape. But jumping in and out, trying to find the BEST TIMES to invest does not work in either the stock market or in a marriage. You must think long-term.

Make long-term commitments at the onset of marriage. Try unique ideas which communicate your intentions for a long and happy union. One husband used jewelry to convey his commitment. On their first wedding anniversary, he gave his wife a silver charm bracelet with a single charm. Each succeeding anniversary, he surprised his wife with a silver charm to commemorate an eventful moment during that particular year—the birth of a child, a favorite trip, a noted accomplishment.

On their Silver 25th Wedding Anniversary, his wife's charm bracelet was an assortment of silver memories. To further illustrate his long-term investment plan, he surprised his wife with a gold bracelet and charm on their 26th anniversary. Now he searches for gold charms and intends for his wife's bracelet to be an accumulation of golden memories on their 50th anniversary. This husband fully understands the value of investing in his wife.

At present, the marriage stock is valued rather low, as indicated by the increasing numbers of divorce. But your SPOUSE still remains a Blue Chip Stock. It is currently undervalued but maintains all the possibilities of unlimited growth.

When investors study the prospectus of a Blue Chip Stock, they realize the importance of stability and look for indications of strong, consistent growth. Your spouse investment can add qualities similar to these to your PLP. If you have selected a Blue Chip spouse, there is little reason to fear that your investment will not yield recognizable dividends as you continue to invest. In fact, you will discover as you invest more and more of your time and effort into your relationship, the dividends will keep getting larger and larger.

Warning! Wise investors understand that even Blue Chips take a tumble once in a while. However, because they know their investments well, they understand the benefits of investing, particularly when their Blue Chip Stocks are low. Because they firmly believe in the future of their investments, they continue to read and study publications which provide indications of their stock's progress. They closely watch their investment while continuing to invest in it. You can apply this same strategy to your marriage.

When you detect that your Blue Chip Spouse is in a slump invest even more time and effort.

When you detect that your Blue Chip Spouse is in a slump, or perhaps is being deflated by unfavorable conditions, this often signals an opportunity to invest even more time and effort. Astute investors recognize the opportunity because they know their investment well. Watch for indications suggesting that your spouse is in need of extra attention. Try investing in your spouse in different ways and at different times. If you need help in finding various ways to invest, visit your public library. Countless publications abound on strengthening relationships and marriage commitment. There are also other sources available.

Seminars provide means of learning better skills in communication. In addition, observe successful older couples who have weathered the storms of a long marriage and basked in the enjoyment of a devoted relationship. They can inspire you and perhaps help you discover new and intriguing investment ideas. But there is an even better way to discover ways to invest. Communicate openly with your spouse.

Investing in your spouse can be easier and much more exciting than investing in a Blue Chip on the market. In the stock market you often have to wait until the market opens to find out how your stock is doing that day. Furthermore, you cannot be assured of accessing up-to-date information when the market is in an upswing or in a downturn.

With your spouse you can find out first thing in the morning how things are going. You do not have to read the paper to see if your spouse has taken a leap or a tumble. Just take time to talk to your spouse. Find out first hand how things are going! Communication is certainly one of the keys to a richer and more prosperous relationship.

In any enterprising and successful business, constant measures are taken to keep the company enticing to the investor. Such motives would help many languishing marriages.

If both partners decided to invest heavily in the marriage relationship, having a common goal to keep it alive and enticing, such a merger would have limitless potential. But how do you keep your marriage appealing and exciting to both partners?

Often it is the consistent, little investments which reap huge dividends. Husbands and wives both require attention. Praise your spouse. When your wife gets all dressed up for a night out, even if it is just to the movies, tell her how attractive she looks. When she wears your favorite perfume, acknowledge her attempt to please you. When she earns recognition in her career, celebrate the occasion together.

For wives, let your husband know he is still attractive, even if his hair line is beginning to recede. Take his hand when you are walking side by side and squeeze it. One small squeeze relays a king-size message that you care.

Be courteous to each other. Never interrupt when your spouse is telling a joke or story. Just enjoy! Laugh together. And laugh at yourself with your spouse. Rejuvenate your marriage. Have fun. Life deals many horrific blows. You will certainly be forced to be serious at times. But if you and your spouse can have fun together, even the serious sides to life will remain in balance.

Invest time in being together. Whether on a mountain watching a breathtaking sunset or scrunching together in a crowded elevator among a throng of people, be together. Make each other the main attraction.

Again, remember to talk. Many young couples fall into the trap of believing a spouse should instinctively know of the other's desires and needs. A marriage relationship does not grow by osmosis. Discuss openly each other's longings and wants. Take a risk and share your dreams.

You might not have similar dreams in many instances and often you will discover your opposite areas. Not only is that natural, but it is also very synergistic. The positive forces each one brings to the relationship enhances and enlarges the individual lives of both partners.

Learn from each other. You have come from different homes, different backgrounds, and sometimes different environments. Each brings positive ideas. Discuss the values and concepts you each hold dear. Then together decide which ones you will nourish in your marriage.

Every company, or marriage, will experience occasional downturns. However, such downturns often lead to contemporary new ideas or methods necessary to spur the company, or the marriage, to new heights. For example, a computer company which suddenly finds its products becoming outdated is often forced to search for state-of-the-art ideas in order to keep the company going. The need to search for innovative ideas and processes can be applied to your marriage.

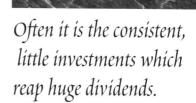

Often it is the consistent, little investments which reap huge dividends.

When your spouse investment begins to fall, incorporate unique ideas into your marriage to keep it prospering. Remember, the wise investor who firmly believes in his vested interests buys more, especially when his Blue Chips are low. In your marriage, a downturn becomes a time of heavy investing. In fact, at times you may have to limit the contributions in other areas of your PLP and concentrate primarily on your spouse.

You might schedule a weekend together, away from children and obligations so you can be free to talk. Attending a seminar on rejuvenating your marriage might be beneficial. Or perhaps all you need is to take a nice, long walk together and talk. Whatever you do, invest. You will suffer a catastrophic loss if you just stand idly by and watch your precious stock crash. So take action!

Another valuable strategy of wise investors is consistent investing. This is also a concept which can be used in your marriage. For example, imagine that you and your spouse decide to choose one day of the week to be "your day." On that special day, you surprise each other with a small gift.

Now forecast what might happen. The first two months are fun. You buy each other little things like chocolates, flowers, T-shirts or stationery. But after two months, you struggle for gift ideas. This is when the real dividends begin to emerge.

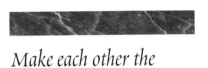

Make each other the main attraction.

You now have cause to listen intently to what your spouse says because an idea for a gift might surface. You note that special day of the week on your PLP worksheet so you won't forget.

Even on hectic and frustrating days, one glance at your PLP calendar reminds you of "your day" and thoughts flash immediately to your spouse.

In a marriage, you should not "need" a reason to think of your spouse. But admit it. When schedules are overloaded and obligations are at a peak, you do not go through the day dreamily thinking of your marriage partner.

After four or five months, you might consider abandoning "your day" and the gift. Thinking of a gift becomes more difficult each week. But consider the returns.

Don't you enjoy taking a few moments to select a gift for that special person? Don't you relish the idea of having one day out of the week "your day?" And quite honestly, don't you enjoy having your spouse surprise you with a gift? It's like a perk in your marriage which only the two of you share.

What do you do if you forget to find a gift for your spouse? There are always the timeless, yet very appreciated, gifts of a back rub, a letter, an evening shared together. Sometimes your gift might be a quick trip to get a treat—just the two of you. No matter the gift, you have reason to be together.

There are added dividends to such an investment. Remember, dividends are excess earnings and profits that are given back to the investor to encourage continued support. Your children will observe your actions. They will delight in seeing their father walk in the door with a smile on his face and a package in his arms for their mother. They will anticipate their mother

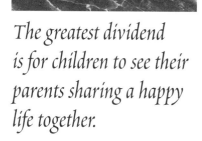

The greatest dividend is for children to see their parents sharing a happy life together.

pulling out a gift for their father. They will be delighted when the gifts are shared with them.

The greatest dividend is for children to see their parents sharing a happy life together. Who knows, they might decide to initiate the same type of investment in their marriage. Everyone loves a gift!

Invest generous amounts of time and effort in your spouse. When one husband was asked what he received for his birthday from his wife of thirty years, he remarked,

"She gave me the best present I could ever ask for. Usually the two of us like to retire very early in the evening. But last night, on my birthday, she stayed up past midnight and we talked and talked. It was the greatest present she could have given me."

Investing time in someone you love can often be more precious than anything you could ever buy at the store. Perhaps Ralph Waldo Emerson said it best:

"Rings and other jewels are not gifts, but apologies for gifts. The only gift is a portion of thyself."

When an investment is made in a spouse, not only does the investor reap huge dividends, but the spouse benefits as well, and the relationship grows stronger. A merger takes place which brings together a partnership of two individual people who develop into a much stronger enterprise than either of them could become on their own.

By consistently investing in this relationship, a valuable account will accrue which will eventually become the inheritance of your children. It is similar to establishing a trust fund, or a legacy left to your heirs in "Memory of Mom and Dad."

Since children were mentioned here as the heirs to your Spouse Investment, it is only logical that they become a part of your PLP.

But first, take a little break and read the following story. You will be amazed to discover how closely your life may relate to that of a farmer.

"RINGS AND OTHER
JEWELS ARE NOT GIFTS,
BUT APOLOGIES FOR
GIFTS. THE ONLY GIFT IS
A PORTION OF THYSELF."

— RALPH WALDO EMERSON

Two Lucky Farmers
A Modern Day Parable

Two Lucky Farmers

*O*nce upon a time there were two very lucky farmers. They were each gifted a large portion of rich, fertile land. Farmer Joe, a most humble man, was extremely grateful for his gift. He arose early the following morning and packed his lunch. He planned to invest his entire day studying the land and assessing its value.

The other farmer, Bill, was very excited about his gift, also. But instead of going to the field, he drove into town. He had to tell everyone about his gift and what a marvelous piece of property it was. He spent a long day in town and when he arrived home late that evening, he was exhausted.

Every day humble Farmer Joe went to his field and made great preparation for his planting. He studied each portion of land carefully. He determined where the weeds would most likely grow so he could snatch them out of the ground before they strangle his little plants. His days were long. But a miracle occurred. He seemed to grow stronger the longer and harder he worked.

While Farmer Joe worked diligently in his field, Farmer Bill sat on his front porch and admired his own land. He often invited friends over so they could also admire the rich, fertile soil. He was so tired from entertaining all of his friends that he found little time to actually work in his field.

The day arrived for the planting. Farmer Joe was well prepared and arose early to gather his seeds. He had purchased only the best seeds he could find. He began to laboriously plant the right seeds in the right places.

Every evening he was so exhausted from his work that he fell into bed early. But the following morning he was up before the sun planting his seeds.

At last his planting was complete. But he continued to go to his field. He made sure that the watering was just right for the different crops. He watched for the weeds which he knew would eventually creep around his plants, trying to destroy them. Before any damage could be done, Farmer Joe was there, pulling the weeds out by their roots and throwing them away.

Farmer Bill, on the other hand, had become so distracted that he had forgotten to purchase his seeds. When he finally drove to town, the finest seeds had been sold. But he rationalized that it really didn't matter how good his seeds were because the soil was rich and fertile.

He hurried home and started to plant. The sun beat down upon him and he became tired and disgruntled. He began tossing the seeds into the wind, hoping they would find fertile places to grow.

That evening as he lay in bed, he thought of the coming months when he would harvest his crops. He was terribly concerned because his tractor and combine were old. He worried that his friends and neighbors would see him out in his beautiful land with machinery that was rusted and battered. He decided that he must allow for more time in town finding new machinery for the harvest. The following morning, he was off to the city again.

Throughout the summer months, humble Farmer Joe faithfully watered and tended his crops. He was astonished at their growth. He continued to pull the weeds. Very few ever lived long enough to harm his budding plants.

Farmer Joe grew to love his land. The more he loved it, the harder he worked to help it produce fine crops.

The day finally arrived for the harvest. Farmer Bill proudly drove his new tractor and combine to his field. With a broad grin on his face, he waved to his neighbors as they drove by. He was ready to harvest his crops in style.

But to his dismay, he could hardly harvest a single bail. His plants were frail and feeble. Weeds had taken root, suffocating and strangling his precious crops.

As he contemplated his circumstances, Farmer Bill became angry and bitter. He noticed his neighbor, Farmer Joe, and his bounteous crops.

"I was cheated," he sneered. "Why was my neighbor given better land than I?"

Farmer Bill sat atop his new tractor, shaking his fist furiously, while humble Farmer Joe continued to work diligently in his field. He did not even notice his angry neighbor. He was too busy gathering his harvest.

5

PARENT INVESTMENT

*W*hen you invest in the Parent Stock, your valuable commodity is your children. You become a great deal like a farmer. Why? Because when your children are young, you are constantly teaching them, which is similar to a farmer planting seeds in fertile soil.

Once you become a parent, you begin to realize there are so many things you must teach—so many seeds to plant. Chances are you will become overwhelmed with your responsibility. In order to offset discouragement, you might study the age-old antics of wise farmers.

They cultivate the ground early in the spring. The reason for cultivating is to till the earth so it is in prime condition to receive and nourish the seeds. Likewise, you prepare your children beginning at birth for the time when you will plant worthwhile ideas. You will nurture and love and build a trusting relationship. When it is time to plant seeds of learning, your child will be prepared to receive those concepts which you hope will grow and mature.

As the farmer plants his seeds with faith of harvesting a bounteous crop, you plant values and concepts, with similar faith that your child will mature into a responsible individual who displays integrity and other virtues. But how do you keep from becoming disheartened as you view the future of endless planting?

You take one day at a time and enjoy each season of cultivating, planting and harvesting, much like a farmer.

Each spring, dedicated farmers experience renewed vitality and vigor as they view their land and anticipate beginning anew to cultivate and prepare the soil for planting time. Their anticipation heightens as they envision a bountiful harvest.

You must decide whether you will invest your time and efforts in planting worthwhile seeds or spend the time scattering menial seeds with little anticipation of a rewarding harvest.

As a parent, you will receive much joy when you harvest the satisfaction of watching your child put to use values you taught. After that harvest, it is time to again prepare your child for another planting season. You will begin to understand the age-old wisdom of cultivating, planting and harvesting which continues throughout your lifetime.

But how does the analogy of farming and parenting pertain to "investing" in your child?

You must decide whether you will invest your time and efforts in planting worthwhile seeds or spend the time scattering menial seeds with little anticipation of a rewarding harvest.

Just like Farmer Joe, in order to reap a bounteous harvest, you must invest long hours in the field. You must learn how to cultivate. You must know when to plant. And once the seeds are planted, you must continue to nourish and care for your child so your teachings can grow and mature. However, there will be obstacles along the way.

Many noxious weeds will emerge, such as immoral books, indecent movies, and even destructive peer pressure. They will try to strangle and suffocate your growing plants. But if you are in the field, keeping watch, you can pluck out many weeds before they do much harm. Note, being in the field is an invaluable way to invest.

Remember that investing is putting time to a use with hope of a profit (or harvest). If you merely spend, or pass time with your children, you will most likely be unaware of most harmful weeds. Does this mean you are to be in the field twenty-four hours a day?

Not at all. You want your child to grow strong and develop the capacity to make wise decisions. This will not happen if you are hovering over your child and being overly protective. Your child will grow stronger and wiser if given the chance to display strength and fortitude against negative forces. Consider this true account.

A wise father recognized that much of the material in movies and television was inconsistent with the values he tried to instill in his children. He invested much time and effort in teaching them the negative aspects of viewing such material. Nevertheless, he knew he could not be with his children in every instance to help them decide wisely what they should watch. The decision was theirs.

One evening, his daughter arrived home after being out with her friends. She was grinning. "Dad, you should be so proud of me," she boasted. "One of the girls put in a video I knew you wouldn't want me to watch. So I grabbed one of my friends and we went outside and played basketball in the driveway. We had a great time!"

Investing in children requires a long-term perspective, much like the Spouse Investment.

Such immediate dividends will not always be recognized when investing in your children. However, there are usually sufficient returns to encourage further investments, thus helping you to maintain an INVESTMENT ATTITUDE.

Investing in children requires a long-term perspective, much like the Spouse Investment. You must be able to persevere through the inevitable ups and downs.

Presently, the Parent Investment might not be too appealing due to the overall conditions of society. Juvenile crime, teen pregnancy, and gangs have created terrible market conditions. But long-term investors know that when the market is low they should invest even more.

Consider your children your Growth Stocks. Growth Stocks are an aggressive investment, with the main objective being long-term growth rather then immediate income. Your children have all the possibility of unlimited growth. They are merely in embryo of what they may become.

How risky is the Parent Investment? Very! When children are young and maturing, they experience many upturns and downturns. You must be courageous.

Parenting is a volatile investment. How many parents are prepared for the incredible anxiety which occurs when "goos" and "gurgles" of an angelic newborn escalate into screams and cries of pain from colic? How many inexperienced parents shudder at the sudden change in personality when little "stocks" try to exhibit independence? The truth is, there are many stages through which your child must pass in order to mature. But don't let this frighten you. Your parents survived, and so will you.

Your children have all the possibility of unlimited growth. They are merely in embryo of what they may become.

Once you have decided to invest in this area, you might wonder how to invest in your children? There are so many things you can do. A couple of young mothers learned that love is one of the key factors.

Two sisters-in-law, who were more like sisters, were extremely committed to finding different ways of investing in their children. Since their children were of similar ages, when one discovered a new class or a new team sport, she called the other mother and they heavily weighed the advantages and disadvantages. Their main concern was providing stimulating experiences so their children would develop positive character traits.

Suddenly, tragedy struck and one of the mothers contracted a terminal disease and died within months. The remaining young mother was devastated. She lost not only her best friend but also her colleague in rearing children.

Saddened and grieving, she reflected upon the many events they had shared with their families. Through all the sport competitions and music and dance recitals, they had made some wise investments in behalf of their children. While recalling all the activities and fun, one compelling statement of her sister-in-law echoed in her mind--"The most important thing you can do for your children is to love them."

If you learn to love being with your children, you will grow to love them.

Although the statement is simple, it carries a compelling message. And it is something which every parent has the capacity to do. If you learn to love being with your children, you will grow to love them.

There are many ways to learn how to love being with your children. Join in their activities and invite them to join in yours.

One young woman loved to bake. When she became a parent, she placed her infant in a carrier which was centered on the kitchen counter while she prepared appetizing dishes. As other children were added, they also became a part of the mother's baking team.

As they baked breads and cookies and giggled while they mixed and tasted the dough, many memories were created. When her oldest child decided he needed a bike, his mother suggested they bake goodies for him to sell so he could help buy himself a bicycle.

As her little boy sold his baked goods, neighbors and friends enjoyed the treats so much that they asked for the recipes. Delighted at such a response, the young mother gathered her children around and asked if they would like to create a cookbook with their own recipes inside.

Eventually, that little home-made cookbook bound with tassels of brightly colored yarn, became a part of many of the neighborhood kitchens. It even caught the attention of a publisher and was published.

At the very beginning when the young mother placed her first newborn on the kitchen counter, she did so because she wanted her child at her side. An incredible bond of love between parent and child was forged as they shared many hours together. Each succeeding child magnified

Decorate your home with pictures of your child.

the love created in their kitchen. That mother never imagined that by making such a small investment with each child, someday she and her children would reap the exciting dividend of seeing their home-made cookbook in local bookstores.

Such dividends usually add to a child's self-esteem. But there are countless other ways in which to help your child feel good inside. One such idea is to decorate your home with pictures of your child.

Photograph moments of your child being together with you, with siblings, or on family outings. Display pictures which preserve priceless memories. Enlarge story-telling photographs and hang them on your walls. The pictures relay the messages to your child: "You are important!" "You belong to people who love you!"

No doubt, you have heard the statement that one picture is worth a thousand words. What a great investment if each displayed photo communicates a thousand times the message, "You are loved!" Very few investments reap such high returns.

Another investment which promises similar successful prospects is that of reading books together. With an INVESTMENT ATTITUDE, no longer will you neglect reading bedtime stories. Your desire for continued growth in your child entices you to invest valued time in this area. The forging of bonds, the introduction of the wonderful world of reading, the gift of intelligence, the moments of teaching—these are but a few rich bonuses awaiting you.

If you don't believe that reading to your children is a wise investment, study Jim Trelease's book, *The New Read-Aloud Handbook.* He will convince you that reading to your children is one of the most valuable investments you will ever make.

The author recognizes that you might not understand how to begin such an investment. So he makes it easy. He lists quality books that will capture the interest of children of all ages. He maintains that a successful reading program begins with parents willing to invest in their children.

Trelease admonishes parents, "At the very start, you should understand the costs involved. Public library cards are free and therefore the most expensive and beautiful children's books in the world are yours, free for a lifetime. There are no fancy teaching machines to buy for your home or classroom, nothing to plug in, no lesson plans or flashcards. Nor do you need a college or high school diploma to do it. For those who believe it cannot be valuable unless you can order it from a catalogue or buy it at a mall, you're going to be disappointed. The only cost is your time."

You invest MONEY in the stock market. You invest TIME and EFFORT in your children.

Even the slightest investments of notes under pillows, treats after school, or moments on the side of the bed qualify as worthwhile deposits. With an INVESTMENT ATTITUDE, you quickly realize that many simple, everyday experiences are avenues leading to valuable, and fun investment time.

You invest MONEY *in the stock market.* *You invest* TIME *and* EFFORT *in your children.*

Raking the lawn provides the opportunity to jump in the leaves together. Reading a joke book with your child can evolve into moments of joking and laughing together. Going to the beach can lead to an afternoon of building sand-castles and dreams together. Make sure you invest lots of time in these fun areas while your children are young because you are forging bonds which you hope will be strong enough to hold you together for many years to come.

As children grow older, provide opportunities for them to discover their strengths and talents. If they display a love for music, find ways to let them take music lessons. Their appreciation for the fine arts will have an opportunity to develop. They will learn self-discipline as they practice.

Another area which encourages discipline is athletic sports. Encourage them to enroll in team or individual sports which are often offered through your community at very little cost. Here they will learn sportsmanship while mastering new skills.

Attend their events and cheer for them. If you have a video camera, produce a personal video tape for each child. Let them be the "star" of their own movie.

You want your children to feel valuable and important. There are many things you can do which can help you achieve this.

When you speak to your children, look into their eyes. Listen to what they say. Answer when they call your name. Invest time in heart-to-heart talks. Don't let a day go by without expressing your love for them. Teach them skills so they can sense their independence and growth.

Often, many everyday tasks are investing tools which can provide skill training. Take, for example, the chore of preparing meals for your family. Much good can transpire by the kitchen sink.

Invite your children to assist in food preparation. Ask them to set the table, fill the water glasses, peel the carrots. Eventually, the investment time in the kitchen pays high dividends. Your children learn life-coping skills which they will carry with them when leaving for college, professions or marriage. An added bonus is the memories of being with you in the kitchen.

Preparing meals together precedes eating together. Why is it important for families to eat together? You are more likely to take an interest in your children's activities because mealtime provides communication time.

In our hurry-up lifestyle, the commodity of communication is often short-changed. As your children age, you must keep the communication lines open. Why? Because your little toddlers will one day grow into teenagers.

Teenagers often find it difficult to communicate with parents, especially if they seldom interacted earlier. When teens arrive at this stage in their development, they closely relate to cyclical stocks in the financial world. If your children are still very young, you might not feel this applies to you. But before you know it, you will be investing in teenagers.

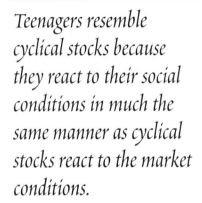

Teenagers resemble cyclical stocks because they react to their social conditions in much the same manner as cyclical stocks react to the market conditions.

Teens can be some of the most terrific and interesting people to be around. Few adults possess the energy and enthusiasm that this age group enjoys. So why do they compare to cyclical stocks as was suggested earlier?

Teenagers resemble cyclical stocks because they react to their social conditions in much the same manner as cyclical stocks react to the market conditions.

When the market rises, cyclical stocks rise. When the market falls, cyclical stocks fall. In much the same manner, teens mimic their peers. Jr. High students often feel more secure when they dress and act like their friends. This is a time when friends may become much more important than family.

Teenagers also struggle with enormous growth both physically and emotionally. Many times your teenager's actions are as puzzling and perplexing to him or her as they are to you. Be patient. Keep investing.

Search for excuses to take your teen with you. Often that involves inviting friends. If you are in a situation where you share carpools with other parents, value the carpooling time.

Usually carpools are a headache. But when you load your car with your teenager and his or her friends, you tune in to what is being said as they turn up the radio.

Invest this time wisely. Have treats in the car because food is a magic highway to a teenager's heart which opens passage-

By the time you have raised your own children, you have earned the right to be classified a GRAND PARENT.

ways for friendshipping. Observe how your teenager interacts with the carpool conversation. If the radio is loud enough and your passengers think you aren't listening, you can learn valuable information about your teen's interests and activities. It's one small way of staying close to your teen.

If your teenager puts on an iron shield and refuses to let you get close, try not to vent your anger. You might become discouraged and decide to invest elsewhere. At those discouraging times, reflect upon your youth. Be honest. Did you always want your parents around? Were you ever embarrassed in their presence? Didn't they seem rather old-fashioned in their views and ideas? Didn't you finally cross that stage of life and evolve into a rather normal, likable human being again?

Chances are, your teen will do likewise. As your teenager gradually emerges out of the cyclical stage of life, your investing will most likely reap some bounteous returns. Those now young adults increase the value of your PLP. They become managers in your account by assisting you in rearing younger children.

Older children greatly influence younger siblings. In fact, many times a younger child takes the advice of an older sibling long before taking the same advice from a parent.

The older children play an enormous role as an example. Hopefully, your investment of quality time and effort will help your first children develop admirable traits and self-confidence which can be passed down to your younger ones. But that is only one of the valuable returns you hope to gain.

Your dreams still may be fulfilled through investing in your grandchildren.

One of the most rewarding dividends of the Parent Investment is when your young adults express independence and maturity and decide to add to their own portfolios by investing in the Spouse Investment for themselves. At this point, your PLP expands with the merger, especially if your child selects a Blue Chip spouse. Further dividends await you.

Down the road you can expect the stock to split and you will become proud grandparents. You will then be glad that you understood the importance of a generous investment in your Parent Stock. You will be grateful for your determination to continue investing during the turbulent years.

Most grandparents agree that nothing quite compares to a grandchild. By the time you have raised your own children and have invested in many portions of life, you feel as though you have earned the right to be classified a Grand Parent.

You will continue an investment in your grandchildren because you more fully understand the value and worth of a child. It is a time for renewed hopes and dreams to burst forth.

Again, you relive the hopes and dreams you once held dear in your youth. Perhaps there was a part of your PLP which never provided the returns you had hoped. Your dreams still may be fulfilled through investing in your grandchildren.

Enjoy your Parent Investment! Consistent investing in this area provides the possibility of unlimited growth and high returns throughout your entire life.

Your PLP is growing. With quality investments in your PERSONAL GROWTH, SPOUSE and PARENTING, your portfolio promises you a rich life. But three investments are not quite enough diversification. Let's consider your CAREER.

6

CAREER INVESTMENT

R emember in third or fourth grade when your teacher asked you to write a paragraph on what you wanted to be when you grew up? You could probably think of so many exciting and interesting careers that it was difficult to decide which one to write about.

However, those childhood aspirations likely faded into reality as you grew older. By the time you graduated from high school, you realized that playing for the Dallas Cowboys or singing on stage with the Rolling Stones was not what you wanted after all. Or perhaps you had to face the cold hard fact that they did not want you.

If you are like most people, this was one of the most exciting, yet frustrating aspects of entering adulthood — the moment you had to decide what you wanted to be. Because you knew this would be an important decision for your future, you wanted to study your options thoroughly so you could make a wise choice in this investment area.

In many ways, an investment in a career can be compared to investing in a Balanced Mutual Fund for your financial portfolio. A Balanced Mutual Fund is a collection of investments

---

which yields different types of returns such as current interest income, dividends and capital appreciation, or growth.

Compare your career to this fund. You may receive a salary as the current income which you need to pay the bills and other necessary living expenses. In addition, you enjoy peri-

Making money is merely a small portion of the benefits available in a successful career.

odic dividends from bonuses and promotions or special recognition for a job well done. You also grow as you continue investing time and effort learning new skills and applying the knowledge you acquire.

Investing in a career probably seems quite fundamental. But how do you select your career and what should you expect to gain from this investment?

Like a wise investor, you must determine your investment objectives and study your options. Today, many children are starting at a very early age to focus on what they want to become when they are older. Most school districts are now preparing Jr. High and High School students to make wise decisions in career planning. Aptitude tests help students recognize individual strengths and weaknesses. Counselors provide information concerning qualifications and aspects of different jobs.

If students desire to go to college, they will be directed to take certain classes which prepare them for college entrance. If they are more inclined for a trade school, they are given advice accordingly.

But even with all the benefits of today's educational programs, many young people still have no idea what they want to be, nor have they considered all of the rewards that can be associated with investing in a successful career. In fact, if you ask them their career objective, the likely response will be, "I want to make a lot of money."

If only students were tutored in an INVESTMENT ATTI-TUDE CLASS! They could learn while they still have youth as a valuable asset that making money is merely a small portion of the benefits available in a successful career. They could be taught to invest their time in something they love to do.

At an early age they could realize the difference between investing their time in class as compared to spending precious moments waiting for the bell to ring. If high school students understood the benefits of investing in their education, the desire to cheat in class and much of the boredom in daily assignments would greatly decrease.

An INVESTMENT ATTITUDE would help them comprehend the correlation between gaining knowledge and skills which are necessary in acquiring self-confidence—a valuable tool necessary in achieving goals and aspirations.

Consider the many advantages of going to college if students were fortified with an INVESTMENT ATTITUDE. Attending class becomes a high priority because of the desire to learn. They do not skip classes nor do they spend their time going to class just to accrue graduation hours. They attack studies and assignments diligently because they expect to reap bounteous returns from their acquired knowledge. All the time, their self-confidence develops and matures. With confidence and newly acquired skills, doors open to new opportunities and new acquaintances which lead to even more investment avenues.

Beginning with elementary school, investing in a career can start many years before you gain employment. You invest—and spend—along the path of career preparation. The sad part is that you often do not realize the full impact of what you are doing. When it is time to choose a career, too many people make the mistake of focusing only on the monetary

With an Investment Attitude, limitless areas are just waiting for you to make a deposit.

rewards by placing too much emphasis on securing a generous salary. Too many do not realize that if you chase after money, chances are you will not catch it. Your career choice should not be based solely upon the desire to accumulate finances. By so doing, you miss out on other rewards which are available.

But what if you were not tutored with an INVESTMENT ATTITUDE in your younger years and you fortunately acquired a successful high salaried position? The exciting fact is that if you understand and apply the INVESTMENT ATTITUDE concept, your current career has all the possibility of becoming even more successful and enjoyable. And you can apply the concept immediately.

Even if you are presently engaged with a prestigious firm or company, chances are you still experience days when your work becomes routine. That does not have to happen. With an INVESTMENT ATTITUDE, limitless areas are just waiting for you to make a deposit.

An INVESTMENT ATTITUDE is mandatory when assigned tasks of attaining skills in a foreign or intimidating area such as learning a new network system or a new computer program.

Deposits of time and effort will accrue many worthwhile returns and dividends.

Never spend your time checking off completed assignments. Each day, *invest* in your challenges with the goal of gaining more knowledge along with the forecast that the more you learn, the more confidence you will gain in your profession. With an INVESTMENT ATTITUDE, you will become a valuable asset to your business. You will also become invaluable to your co-workers.

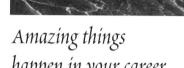

Amazing things happen in your career when money is not the motivation.

Nearly every task, no matter how simple, can lead to meeting new people. Each person provides opportunity for investment. Focus one aspect of your career on making life better for those around you.

Invest time in listening to a co-worker's problem. Really listen. Lend a hand to help someone who is struggling with an assignment. Write a note of comfort to one who is suffering. Make life better for everyone who happens to cross your path.

As you invest time and effort in relationships, you will enjoy many returns and dividends along the course of your career. You will develop personal rapport with mentors who help you gain more knowledge and skill. You will cultivate strong friendships which will become an important part of your PLP. (The investments in friendships will be discussed later in Chapter 7.) You will recognize the fact that amazing things happen in your career when money is not the only motivation.

If you are one of the many people who, at the onset of your career, was most concerned about making money, you have probably made a few discoveries. You now realize that success in most professions depends on how essential you become to your business. Usually the more valuable you are, the higher your salary.

How do you become valuable to your boss and co-workers? You forget yourself and go to work. Even a grouchy supervisor notes when an employee is willing to accomplish more work than was assigned. A co-worker who is struggling with personal or work problems often appreciates an E-mail note of encouragement. Recognize that most people carry some kind of burden. That will keep you from judging or gossiping.

Your money cannot love you back, but the people in whom you invest can.

When you are asked to work long hours or assigned unwanted trips out of town, the ability to forget yourself while forging ahead becomes an invaluable investing tool. A fourteen-hour workload wears everyone out. Invest in a cheerful countenance to help you and everyone else survive. When you step out to grab a late bite at the local deli, buy a treat for everyone. Even a bag of snack-size candy bars will be appreciated and it won't take a chunk out of your budget.

On out-of-town trips, use the evenings to invest in letters to your spouse and children. Read that book you have had to put on hold. Review your PLP and plan future investments. Acquaint yourself with the area and recognize the role your career plays in that community. If your hotel has a gym, invest in a workout. With so many potential investment areas, you have no excuse to spend your time wishing for different circumstances.

Another realization is that money alone does not assure happiness in your work. With an INVESTMENT ATTITUDE, you will find that the rewards associated with contributing to the well-being of those around you often outweigh the monetary gains. Money becomes only one of the many accumulated returns in your profession. You come to understand that a "rich" life is a life abundant with people whom you care about and who care about you. Your money cannot love you back, but the people in whom you invest can!

By focusing only on the monetary aspects of a career, you limit yourself in terms of the many dividends and returns available from this investment.

By focusing only on the monetary aspects of a career, you limit yourself in terms of the many dividends and returns available from this investment.

One way to comprehend wise investing in your career is to study those who have been successful in this area. There is one such gentleman I have observed for many years. You would probably find him as fascinating as I do. To most people he is considered rather wealthy because his financial portfolio boasts of several million dollars.

However, he is a modest man who invested well in many areas of his life, especially in the people around him. You would probably enjoy his company a great deal. While his financial portfolio boasts of his money, he does not. Other than occasionally writing out a personal check for a new car or for a summer home in the mountains, he lives a very ordinary, frugal life. He is content. He rarely speaks of his money or belongings.

He did not begin his life wealthy. In fact, he laboriously worked for minimum wages during the early years of his life. Due to contracting rheumatic fever, he barely advanced through 8th grade and received a limited formal education. By struggling through the school of hard knocks and experience, he gained an understanding of the INVESTMENT ATTITUDE.

Though he earned little money as a young man, he lived on even less and always invested in his future. Gradually, his investments grew into a respectable amount, but few people were aware of his wealth because he seldom mentioned it.

When an opportunity surfaced to enter into a business partnership, he was able to take advantage of the offer. Many onlookers commented about his "good luck." But luck had little to do with his success. Because he had invested wisely in accumulating finances and knowledge and skill as well as investing in the people around him, he was prepared when the right opportunity availed itself.

Over the years he had developed a true investing attitude in both his finances and in his life. His first and wisest investment was a Blue Chip Spouse.

In his younger years while he was saving and investing his earnings, he and his wife had five children. His wife became his greatest asset. She sacrificed many of her wants in order to invest in their future. She also invested heavily in rearing their family.

When it was time to harvest crops, she was willing to work in the fields alongside her husband and children. She often ensured ways of making the almost unattainable possible and made sure their offspring appreciated their father's hard work. Truly, she was, and still is, his most valuable investment.

Regretting his own lack of education, he invested a large portion of their money into funds for future use which eventually provided the means of college degrees for all five children. After graduating from college, some of his children then desired to go into business with him. Recognizing their abilities and the knowledge they had accumulated, he readily opened his arms.

Many non-monetary dividends yield much more satisfaction than a coffer of gold.

His financial investments began to yield high returns as his children applied their skills and knowledge gained through their education. He enjoyed the dividends of watching his new partners grow and develop as they learned the value of hard work. As his children grew, so did his business. And as his business prospered, so did his children. A lifetime of investing certainly paid many rich dividends for him and his family.

Just like this successful gentleman, some of your investment gains may be monetary. But other returns will probably have more intrinsic value, such as the investments in people who are valuable to you, much like his children were to him. As he taught his children and witnessed their growth, he experienced a thrill similar to the satisfaction you can enjoy as you help train new employees and watch them attain their goals. As you climb the ladder of success, always remember how much you appreciated those who helped you. Be willing and eager to reach out and lend a hand to those standing below you on the ladder. Money alone cannot promise happiness or a successful career investment.

You might have chosen a profession which pays little in terms of monetary wealth but provides genuine value to your life and to the lives of others. You do not have to have a huge bank account to be incredibly rich. Wealth is not measured only in terms of money and gold. Recall the earlier suggestion that you consider your wealth in terms of spouse, children, friends, and other personal investments.

Think of the teachers in our country. These dedicated people, who enrich the minds and lives of our children, probably did not choose their professions anticipating the accumulation of substantial amounts of money. But when they see their students grow and mature into fine young citizens of our country, they know they invested their time well. The returns of their investments enrich all our lives, as well as theirs.

Reflect upon the artists and musicians whose works enhance our lives. Many died in obscurity and poverty only to have their work become valuable once it was appreciated.

Investing in life does not always accrue monetary rewards. However, many non-monetary dividends yield much more satisfaction than a coffer of gold.

As an example, consider a woman I know, who recently quit her job at the office in order to pursue a career as a stay-at-home mother.

"CAREER?" you might ask. Note that a career is defined as *progress through life with respect to one's work.*

Chapter 6

You might feel that managing a home and children is not a valid career. But ask any young mother who has chosen to leave a job outside the home and invest her efforts into rearing her children. She could tell you a great deal about managing her own little "family" business.

In her career, progress may not be as detectable as in a nine-to-five job where promotions or raises are frequent. Certificates of achievement along with perks such as vacation time, holiday pay or even lunch breaks usually do not exist. Therefore, this career demands patience as well as perseverance. However, if you are a parent, you will readily admit that there are rewards found in parenting that far outweigh any promotion or raise at the office.

You might not think this career sounds very inviting. But the dedicated mothers who choose to invest their time wisely in this area, know of its value. They are unselfishly investing in the trend-setters and future leaders of our country.

With society in its current state, we could all benefit from more people choosing similar careers that focus on aspects other than monetary rewards. Therefore, you should be happy to know, it is not just mothers who are re-evaluating their career choices. Many people are now discovering that by investing too much of their time and effort at the office, they are missing out on other investment opportunities in life.

A number of prominent, successful male professionals today are restructuring the emphasis they place on their careers. Peter Lynch, the famous financial magnate who steered Magellan, the world's largest mutual fund, into prosperity, is a prime example. He decided to simplify his life and invest more time with his wife and children. He is quoted as saying, "I don't know anyone who wished on his deathbed that he had spent more time at the office."

His quote has become an inspiration for many. They follow Peter Lynch's example of investing more heavily in other portions of their PLP. They have decided to work less, accumulate less and live on less. But they do not intend to become idle and lazy.

Many have opted to simply add new investments to their PLP. They invest more time in community service, religion, children and grandchildren. Many share their intelligence and skills through investing in volunteer programs and helping those who are less fortunate.

However, not everyone is in a situation where they can afford to scale back significantly on the amount of time invested in their job or occupation. After all, we cannot overlook the responsibility of providing a living for ourselves and those who depend on us. But it is important to recognize that there are many things in life more important than money.

Invest wisely in your career. Remember, it is similar to a Balanced Mutual Fund because it maintains the ability of yielding many different types of returns. Your career provides challenge for growth and achievement. If wise investments are made, you should accrue many valuable and satisfying returns.

Another investment in life which adds inestimable wealth is one you are probably already enjoying. To some, this investment seems to fall right into their laps. Others have to develop investment skills in this area in order to assure attainment.

Nevertheless, it is an investment worth making. Sometimes this investment alone can hedge your portfolio from the risks of bankruptcy. For this reason, you must consider this investment "as good as gold."

Note that many financial investors include gold in their portfolio because they know if the market were to crash, gold is more likely to remain stable or perhaps even increase in value. Keep this in mind as you read about this next investment.

Enjoy the next chapter. In fact, share it with a FRIEND

$\mathcal{M}$ILES MAY
SEPARATE AND YEARS
MAY FADE RECOLLECTIONS,
BUT WARM AND LOVING
MEMORIES BETWEEN FRIENDS
BAR ALL DISTANCE
AND TIME.

7

ꞋFRIENDS ꞋINVESTMENT

*"Friends are like gold coins in a
rich man's pocket."*

*W*hen life throws an unexpected curve and your
PLP takes a tumble, a sound investment in this
area will reap untold dividends. Miles may separate and years
may fade recollections, but warm and loving memories
between friends bar all distance and time.

Take a moment and recall a dear friend who has played a
major role in your life. Wouldn't you like to visit with that person? Even if it has been several years, you would most likely
resume a conversation right where you left off the last time
you were together.

Most of us would agree that investments in friendships can
be an invaluable part of a PLP.

You may have heard the unbelievable story of Anne
Scheiber. She earned a respected and admired name among the
top investors in our country. Beginning with only $5,000, she
managed to create a fortune of $22 million by the time she
passed away at the age of 101.

Her dazzling return averaged 22.1% a year. What an investor! Many might suggest that she came by most of her fortune through means of an enormous inheritance. But that is not the case.

Anne was one of nine children. Her father died young and her mother had to go to work to support the family. Her brothers were educated, but the girls were not. Anne went to work as a bookkeeper, and she finally put herself through school.

She became a top auditor at the IRS. Anne learned from other people's tax returns that the best way to get rich in America was to invest in stocks.

She was frugal. Her clothes were threadbare and her living expenses were meager. Instead of *spending* her money, she *invested* it.

Every investment meant a lot to Anne and she kept current on the progress of each one. She knew how to diversify her financial portfolio and she understood the importance of constant review for growth.

But Anne made a mistake. She forgot to invest in her life. She never married. According to some accounts, she never even had a sweetheart. Her love in life was investing in money.

Frank Lalli writes, "She died without one real friend; she didn't get even one phone call during her last five years of life." (MONEY, January 1996)

What a tragedy to go through life without having someone else with whom to share it. Hopefully, this story will inspire you to want to build friendships with those around you.

Small investments of long-distance phone calls or short notes and cards slipped in the mail can keep your friendship investment viable no matter how many miles separate. It does not take much.

For your friends living close by, don't forget to call and visit. You might wish to take a gift. Whether it be a flower, a card, a prayer in your heart, or your mere presence, it really doesn't matter. What matters is your caring.

Be selective in choosing your friends for your PLP. Golden are the friends who understand and never complain when your schedule is hectic and they've not heard from you.

Those types of friends always listen but never pry. They offer wise and loving advice only when requested. They provide support and love when one of your other investments takes a tumble. They revel in your triumphs and shed tears with you when you cry. Their valued friendship reminds you that life is good.

An investment in friends teaches many valuable lessons concerning wise investing. Not all stocks are meant for your PLP. Different friends meet different needs. Select those friends who add to the value of your personal life. Likewise, you will do the same to their personal portfolios.

Some friends qualify because of innate abilities which comply with your personality. You feel comfortable just being around them. Many of those people slip almost automatically into your PLP because you simply like them and want them to be a part of your life. Other friends meet your need for growth. They challenge you to reach higher, work harder, accomplish more than you dared dream possible. They are the wind beneath your wings.

Some friends bring out almost dormant traits in your personality. They have a knack of reminding you to laugh more, grumble less and focus on the positive.

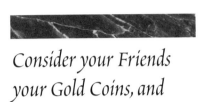

Consider your Friends your Gold Coins, and your life will be rich.

You select some friends because they relate to your present situation in life. You can discuss personal concerns without worry of the conversation going any further.

When you are young and investing heavily in your Personal Growth, Spouse, Children and Career, you might not consider an investment in Friends to be as important as other investment areas. But contemplate your future.

In years to come, other investment needs will alter giving you more time to invest in friends. It is no fun to travel alone, golf alone, or laugh and cry alone.

By investing in Friends when young, you will reap dividends throughout your lifetime. Remember to consider your Friends your Gold Coins, and your life will be rich.

8

CONCLUSION

*Y*ou might have in mind other investments for your PLP. Good for you. You understand that investing in life is a very individual matter.

Hopefully, some of the ideas presented within these pages have served as springboards for you to now begin your Personal Life Investment Plan.

Wherever you go, whomever you meet, whatever you do, with an INVESTMENT ATTITUDE, you will discover a rich and productive life. In financial planning, you are advised to constantly review investments and update them according to your current status. When you are young, you are advised to invest more heavily in stocks. The risk is greater but your portfolio can absorb losses better when you are young than when you are nearing retirement and must rely on your investments to pay your bills.

When you are older, you are advised to keep a certain percentage in cash for emergencies and a smaller portion in stocks. You might invest more heavily in high grade bonds and treasury notes or other lower risk investments. Constant review will maintain a balanced financial portfolio.

Your PLP also requires updating. When you are young, you will probably invest heavily in your career portion. As you marry and add children, you will invest heavily in those areas, while maintaining a sizable investment in your career. When you grow older and children leave, you will redistribute investments once again to meet your needs.

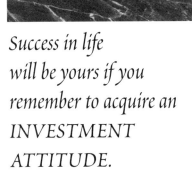

Success in life will be yours if you remember to acquire an INVESTMENT ATTITUDE.

By constantly reviewing and updating your PLP, you will lower the risk of poor investing in any one area. You should be able to manage a balanced life, one filled with accomplishment, satisfaction and happiness.

You will exercise with renewed vigor and stimulate your mind and spirit because you are investing and creating a wealth of PERSONAL GROWTH.

A walk with your SPOUSE will take on new meaning as you hold hands and savor each moment. You will sense a surge of growth in your relationship.

When it's your turn to tend your CHILDREN, you will transform those moments into building blocks of wise investment time.

When you are at the office, your daily routines and personal relationships will arise as new investment avenues for growth and accomplishment in your CAREER.

If you happen to greet an old FRIEND, you will savor the moment because you are investing in a valuable commodity which has promise of many gratifying returns.

Remember, life has its ups and downs, much like the stock market. But if you diversify your Personal Life Portfolio and select wise investments, you will enjoy many rich returns and dividends.

A life of investing is a life of wonderment. There is no limit as to how much you can acquire because you are pursuing:

AN INVESTMENT OF A LIFETIME!

*W*HEREVER YOU GO,

WHOMEVER YOU MEET,

WHATEVER YOU DO, WITH AN

INVESTMENT ATTITUDE, YOU

WILL DISCOVER A RICH AND

PRODUCTIVE LIFE.

$\mathcal{A}$PPENDIX

*T*HIS APPENDIX INCLUDES
INSTRUCTIONS ON HOW TO SET UP
YOUR PERSONAL LIFE PORTFOLIO (PLP)
WORKSHEET. EXAMPLES OF THREE
INDIVIDUALS' WORKSHEETS ARE
PROVIDED FOR REFERENCE AS YOU BEGIN
ESTABLISHING YOUR PERSONAL LIFE
INVESTMENT PROGRAM.

Instructions for
Personal Life Portfolio (PLP) Worksheet

NOTE: *Before you begin writing on your blank PLP Worksheet, make at least one photo-copy to preserve as the blank master copy. If you need additional copies of the PLP Worksheet, please contact Horizon Investments.*

1. DETERMINE YOUR OVERALL INVESTMENT GOAL. Your investment goal for your PLP should state your objectives and how you intend to achieve them. Write your goal in the space provided under Investment Goal at the top of your PLP Worksheet. If you need help constructing your investment goal, it may be helpful to refer to chapter 2 and the examples on the proceeding pages.

2. FORECAST YOUR INVESTMENT RESULTS. Your forecast should explain what you hope to gain from maintaining an INVESTMENT ATTITUDE. Record your forecast in the space provided under Investment Forecast. Again, investment forecast examples are provided in chapter 2 and in the sample PLP Worksheets on the following pages.

3. LIST YOUR AREAS OF INVESTMENT. Under the Investments column of your PLP Worksheet, list the areas or roles in your life that you consider important areas of investment. As discussed in chapters 2 & 3, you may want to list your personal growth investment in the first box to remind you of its importance to your portfolio. Examples of other possible investment areas are provided in sample PLP Worksheets and throughout the book.

4. ESTABLISH SPECIFIC GOALS FOR EACH INVESTMENT. Each investment should have a corresponding goal which expresses your objective of investing in that particular area. Write these goals next to their respective investments under the Goals column of your PLP Worksheet.

---

5. MAKE PHOTOCOPIES OF YOUR PLP WORKSHEET. Once you have recorded your investment goals and forecasts, and listed your investment areas with their corresponding goals, you now have a working copy of your PLP Worksheet. Because the information you have entered thus far will not change on a weekly basis, you can reproduce copies of your worksheet at this point to use for recording your weekly investment activities. As your goals, forecasts and investment areas change periodically, you can simply create a new working copy from the blank master copy you preserved at the start.

6. RECORD THE DATE. On one of the working copies of your PLP Worksheet, record the current date in the space provided after "Week of:" directly above the Goals column. Then record the appropriate date in the space directly below the appropriate day, i.e. Sunday, Monday, Tuesday, etc.

7. PLAN YOUR INVESTING ACTIVITIES FOR THE WEEK. On the working copy for the coming week, record the appointments, meetings, and other activities you have planned in the appropriate box for each day. You will find that many activities fit into more than one investment category, so record them in all that are appropriate. You will discover many areas fill up quickly, while others are left quite blank. As you plan, try to think of ways you can invest in the areas that have the least amount of activities projected for the week.

8. REVIEW YOUR INVESTING ACTIVITIES DAILY. At the start of each day, review your PLP Worksheet to remind you of the areas you desire to invest in for the day. This daily review will help you develop and maintain an INVESTMENT ATTITUDE in everything you do.

9. RECORD ANY UNPLANNED INVESTING ACTIVITIES FOR THE DAY. As you go through each day, you will encounter many activities and opportunities you do not have planned on your PLP Worksheet. At

the end of each day, evaluate which investment areas these activities fit into and record them in the appropriate boxes.

10. REVIEW AND RATE YOUR INVESTING ACTIVITIES FOR THE WEEK. At the end of the week your PLP Worksheet should be quite full. Review each investment area in terms of the activities you listed in the corresponding row. Evaluate how well you invested in each area and then rate yourself in terms of how well you invested in each investment area on a scale of 0 to 6, a 6 being the highest score and a 0 being the lowest. Record your rating in the far right column under IR (Investment Rating). Evaluate your scores and determine which areas may require additional investing for the coming week.

You are now ready to begin planning for the next week!

By using your PLP Worksheet to plan and evaluate each week, you will find yourself enjoying a life of investing in what matters most to you. The INVESTMENT ATTITUDE will permeate everything you do to make your life richer and more rewarding. By consistently utilizing the investing concepts you have been taught, you will be on your way to the most exciting and rewarding investment plan you have ever considered. Welcome to the world of investing ... Investing in Life!

HORIZON INVESTMENTS, L.C.
P. O. Box 1284
Bountiful, Utah 84011-1284
(801) 294-4430

PERSONAL LIFE PORTFOLIO

INVESTMENT GOAL

I will invest my time wisely in the areas of life which are most important to me. Every week I will evaluate my results and realize the areas in which I must invest more time. I will be enthusiastic with each investment whether it reaps a dividend or suffers a downturn. I will maintain an "Investment Attitude" in my daily living.

WEEK OF:	AUGUST 25, 1996	SUNDAY	MONDAY
INVESTMENT	GOALS	8/25	8/19
Personal Growth	*I will exercize my mind, body and spirit on a daily basis. I will not neglect my mental, physical and spiritual growth.*	• Pray • Read • Church • Sunday Walk	• Pray • 30-Min. Workout
Wife	*I will love and support Jim in all he does. I will help make his life more pleasant. He will be my "Blue Chip" investment.*	• Church • Family Time • Sunday Dinner • Sunday Walk	• Call Jim • Review Bank Statement • Dinner
Mother	*I will constantly strive to set a good example for our children. I will help build each child's self-esteem and confidence and maintain a feeling of love within our home.*	• Church • Family Time • Bible Stories • Melissa's hair • Kid's homework	• Kid's car-pool • Jenny - Dance • Homework • Dinner • Melissa - Reading
Job	*I will help financially support our family. I will search for new challenges at work and build close relationships with those around me.*		• Dr. Weller (ins. claims) • Billings Report
Friend	*I will strengthen existing friendships and seek out opportunities to create new friends. I will look for the good in other people.*	• Church (O'Neil's, Perkins, Talbots)	
Sister/ Daughter	*I will maintain a close relationship with my mother and father and my brothers and sisters and their families.*	• Call Mom & Dad	• Jake's B-Day (Call & Mail Present)

INVESTMENT FORECAST

The investments I make today will yield valuable dividends in years to come because I have selected quality "Blue Chip" investments with unlimited potential. My life will be rich and abundant because it will be focused on people rather than on things.

TUESDAY	WEDNESDAY	THURSDAY	FRIDAY	SATURDAY	IR
8/20	8/21	8/22	8/23	8/24	
Pray Read at Lunch	• Pray • Walk	• Pray • Health-Rider	• Pray	• Pray • Exercise • Read	5
	• Meet Jim for Lunch • Dinner	• "OUR DAY" • Jim's Treat	• Date Night (Dinner/Movie) • Call Jim	• Dinner (CC) • Groceries • Football Game • Yard Work	6
Football Practice (Pick up Brad & Friends) Homework After-School Treat (Melissa)	• PTA Meeting • Brad - Scouts • Shopping - (Jenny & Melissa) • Homework	• Homework • Piano	• Gymnastics (Car-pool)	• Brad - Practice Game • Yard Work • Dinner (Country Club)	6
Payables Processing Lunch with Joan 2nd Review		• JPM Check • Tammy's B-Day • A/P • Run Report	• Call Fran Thompson		5
Lunch w/ Joan Call Kay	• Visit Ruth C.			• Football Game (Colemans)	4
	• E-mail Robert & Kim				4

INVESTMENT GOAL

I will learn to invest in life and no longer spend my time & effort. I will strive to maintain an "investment attitude" in everything I do. I will diversify my investments in life and allocate my resources to the areas in my life that matter most.

WEEK OF:	APRIL 18, 1997	SUNDAY	MONDAY
INVESTMENT	GOALS	4/18	4/19
Personal Growth	*Grow spiritually, physically & mentally. Plan my week and put the most important things in life first.*	• Read • Plan week (PLP) • Relax	• Meditate • Rollerblade Jog • Read I.O.L.
Spouse	*Invest time & effort in making Karen's life more pleasant. Show her I love her.*	• Breakfast • Family Time • Evening Walk	• Work (job) • Rollerblade Jog • Hogi-Yogi Night (ice cream)
Parent	*Help my children realize their full potential. Show them I love them through my actions and my words.*	• Breakfast • Family Time • Jamie - Bed Time Story	• Car Pool (Kristi) • Hogi-Yogi • Help w/Aaron's Homework
Career	*Provide an adequate living for my family. Acquire knowledge & skills to help me be my "own boss" someday.*	• Call Jerry	• Review STF Documents • Staff Mtg. • Apply for Mgt. Semin
Friend	*Develop and strengthen relationships with friends. Uplift them and show my appreciation to them.*	• Call Jerry	• Call Brad Stevens

INVESTMENT FORECAST

By investing in life, I will be able to prioritize those things that matter most to me. My life will become more rich with relationships and I will feel good about what I accomplish each day. My life will be less stressful, because I realize I am in control of what I invest my time and effort in.

TUESDAY	WEDNESDAY	THURSDAY	FRIDAY	SATURDAY	IR
4/20	4/21	4/22	4/23	4/24	
Guitar Class Study Group	• Meditate • Tennis w/ Jim	• Meditate • Read Richest Man in Babylon • Workout@Gym • Computer Class	• Dentist Appointment	• House Repairs (exercise) • Grocery Store • Read/Relax	6
Work Dinner	• Work • Karen-gift • Cook Dinner	• Work • Meet Karen for Lunch	• Work • Date Night (Dinner & Movie)	• House Repairs • BBQ @ Park • Shopping • Kristi's School Play	6
Bed Time Story Cook Dinner	• Aaron's Baseball Game • Bed Time Story • Cook Dinner	• Help w/Homework (Aaron & Kristi)	• Write Check for kids' piano lessons	• Baseball Game (Aaron) • Kristi's Play • BBQ @ Park • Fix Kristi's car	6
Install new software prog. Update Jamison on SPDX proj. Lunch w/ Ted	• Equip. Research • Cost Analysis • TLC Meeting	• Computer Class • Call Boyd (LTM) • Meeting w/Chase • Donnely Stmts.	• Contact KBU • Review TMX Contract w/ Sue • Schedule Meeting w/ LOC		6
Study Group Lunch w/ Ted	• Tennis w/ Jim	• Gym (Jim & Terry) • Computer Class (Hal)		• Smiths (Baseball Game)	5

PERSONAL LIFE PORTFOLIO

INVESTMENT GOAL

I will invest my time and effort instead of spending it. I will remember the importance of investing in many different areas of my life to maintain a balance that will sustain me through life's ups and downs. I will make a conscious effort to invest my time and effort in all I do.

WEEK OF:	APRIL 21, 1996	SUNDAY	MONDAY
INVESTMENT	GOALS	4/21	4/22
Personal Growth	*Maintain a healthy body by exercising and eating right. Focus on what is most important in life.*	• Pray • Church • Read Scriptures	• Pray • Rollerblade
Husband	*Focus on Jill's needs. Recognize her accomplishments and show her I love her by what I do and what I say.*	• Church • Sunday Picnic	• Baskin-Robbins • Jill- gift (congrats for new job)
Student	*Learn all I can from those who know more. Study & apply what I learn at school to my personal life and work.*	• Inv. 631 HW • Strategy-Paper • Writing Assign.	• School • Invst HW • Wrtg Paper
Church/ Community Service	*Invest in serving others. Volunteer time to help neighbors & members of congregation.*	• Church	• DSNN Nigh
Job	*Provide income for Jill & me to live on. Build relationships at work, and create a network that will help my career progress.*		
Brother/ Son	*Invest in family members. Keep relationships with Mom/ Dad & Brother/ Sisters alive & active.*	• Dinner- Mom & Dad • Call Scott • Cori's Address	

INVESTMENT FORECAST

Because I strive to maintain an "Investment Attitude" I will not lose focus on what is most important to me in life. My life will be more peaceful and less stressful because I will maintain a long-term outlook rather than searching for short-term returns. I will discover the rewards associated with investing in others rather than in things.

TUESDAY	WEDNESDAY	THURSDAY	FRIDAY	SATURDAY	IR
4/23	4/24	4/25	4/26	4/27	
• Pray • Exercise	• Pray	• Pray • Rollerblade	• Pray	• Pray • Mtn. Biking	4
• Work		• Work • Rollerblade	• Work • Dinner Date • Video	• BBQ @ park • Biking • Movie	5
• School • Homework (investments) • Work (SDC)	• School • Invst Test • Mgt 680-Case • Business Plan	• Work (SDC)	• Work (SDC)	• Homework (strategy & writing)	6
• Visit Johnson Family				• BBQ @ park	3
• SDC • Clean up • Meals • HCC	• Business Plan • Entr. Class	• SDC • Updates	• SFC • Stonewall project		4
• Kelli- Drill Team	• E-mail Mom from school				5

BIBLIOGRAPHY

Covey, Stephen R. *The 7 Habits of Highly Effective People*. New York, New York. Simon and Shuster, 1990.

Emerson, Ralph Waldo. *Adventures in American Literature*. "Gifts." Harcourt, Brace and Company.

Lalli, Frank. "How She Turned $5,000 into $22 Million." *Money*. January, 1996.

Peale, Dr. Norman Vincent. *The Power of Positive Thinking*. Prentice-Hall, Inc., 1952.

Kushner, Harold S. "Biggest Mistake I Ever Made." *Reader's Digest*. July, 1991.

New Webster's Dictionary and Thesaurus of the English Language. Lexicon Publications, Inc. Danbury, Ct. 1992.

Robbins, Anthony. *Unlimited Power*. Ballantine Books. 1986.

Trelease, Jim. *The New Read-Aloud Handbook*. Penguin Books. 1982.

University of California at Berkeley Wellness Letter. "Wellness Facts." Vol.11. June, 1995.